T0360475

Affect in Organization and Management

Affect in Organization and Management asks how affect theory understands everyday working lives through embodied, social and political practice. Discussing a range of dimensions and perspectives on affect, the book considers how subjects are formed through their connections with others, both human and non- or more-than-human.

The six women writers on affect presented in this series (Sara Ahmed, Kathleen Stewart, Donna Haraway, Jane Bennett, Karen Barad and Rosalyn Diprose) all speak to important themes in organization studies, including power, politics and ethics. Each chapter explores how these thinkers have already influenced organization scholars, as well as how their work can extend our understanding of pressing organizational issues around gender, race, the environment, leadership and ethics. Feminism is a core feature of this collection, highlighting feminist writing with affective, connected and intersubjective possibilities.

Each woman writer is introduced by experts on affect and organization studies. The chapters also suggest further reading and accessible resources. The book is suitable for students, academics and practitioners in business and management, organization studies and critical management studies who want to think differently about organizations.

Carolyn Hunter is Senior Lecturer at the York Management School, University of York, UK.

Nina Kivinen is Associate Professor at the Department of Civil and Industrial Engineering, Uppsala University, Sweden.

Routledge Focus on Women Writers in Organization Studies

Series Note

Given that women and men have always engaged in and thought about organizing, why is it that core management texts are dominated by the writing of men? This series redresses the neglect of women in organization thought and practice and highlights their contributions. Through a selection of carefully curated short-form books, it covers major themes such as structure, rationality, managing, leading, culture, power, ethics, diversity and sustainability; and also attends to contemporary debates surrounding performativity, the body, emotion, materiality and postcoloniality. Individually, each book provides stand-alone coverage of a key sub-area within organization studies, with a contextual series introduction written by the editors. Collectively, the titles in the series give a global overview of how women have shaped organizational thought.

Routledge Focus on Women Writers in Organization Studies will be relevant to students and researchers across business and management, organizational studies, critical management studies, gender studies and sociology.

Rethinking Culture, Organization and Management
Edited by Robert McMurray and Alison Pullen

Morality, Ethics and Responsibility in Organization and Management
Edited by Robert McMurray and Alison Pullen

Affect in Organization and Management
Edited by Carolyn Hunter and Nina Kivinen

For more information about this series, please visit: www.routledge.com/Routledge-Focus-on-Women-Writers-in-Organization-Studies/book-series/RFWWOS

Affect in Organization and Management

Edited by Carolyn Hunter
and Nina Kivinen

NEW YORK AND LONDON

First published 2023
by Routledge
605 Third Avenue, New York, NY 10158

and by Routledge
4 Park Square, Milton Park, Abingdon, Oxon, OX14 4RN

Routledge is an imprint of the Taylor & Francis Group, an informa business

Library of Congress Cataloging-in-Publication Data

Names: Hunter, Carolyn, 1984- editor. | Kivinen, Nina,
    1974- editor.
Title: Affect in organization and management/edited by Carolyn
    Hunter, Nina Kivinen.
Description: New York, NY: Routledge, 2023. | Includes
    bibliographical references and index.
Identifiers: LCCN 2022023309 | ISBN 9781032023199
    (hardback) | ISBN 9781032023205 (paperback) |
    ISBN 9781003182887 (ebook)
Subjects: LCSH: Affect (Psychology) | Psychology, Industrial. |
    Organizational behavior.
Classification: LCC HF5548.8 A595 2022 | DDC 158.7—dc23/
    eng/20220607
LC record available at https://lccn.loc.gov/2022023309

ISBN: 978-1-032-02319-9 (hbk)
ISBN: 978-1-032-02320-5 (pbk)
ISBN: 978-1-003-18288-7 (ebk)

DOI: 10.4324/9781003182887

Typeset in Bembo
by Apex CoVantage, LLC

Contents

List of Contributors   ix

1 **Introduction: Affect in Organization
   and Management**   1
   CAROLYN HUNTER AND NINA KIVINEN

2 **Sara Ahmed: A Return to Emotions**   12
   BONTU LUCIE GUSCHKE, JANNICK FRIIS CHRISTENSEN
   AND THOMAS BURØ

3 **In the Worlding of Kathleen Stewart:
   Daydreaming a Conversation With 'SHE'**   29
   SILVIA GHERARDI

4 **In the Web of the Spider-Woman: Towards a
   New Cosmopolitics of Familiarity and Kinship
   in Organization (Donna Haraway)**   45
   LINDSAY HAMILTON

5 **Jane Bennett: Marvelling at a World
   of Vibrant Matter**   61
   JUSTINE GRØNBÆK PORS

6 **Becoming With Barad: A Material-Discursive-
   Affective Conversation**   76
   NOORTJE VAN AMSTERDAM, KATRINE MELDGAARD KJÆR AND
   DIDE VAN ECK

7 **Corporeal Ethics in the More-Than-Human World (Rosalyn Diprose)** 92

VEERA KINNUNEN

Index 108

Contributors

Noortje van Amsterdam is an Assistant Professor at Utrecht School of Governance. Her research focuses on embodiment and health in organizations, specifically addressing experiences related to gender, ability, age and size. She often uses arts-based methodologies to explore the affective and material aspects of workplace in- and exclusions.

Thomas Burø, Copenhagen Business School, is into ecological thought and organization. His research is inquiring into the ways in which political economy, cultural politics, identity, the pragmatics of aesthetic practice and the patterns of cultural use effectively shape and reshape, regulate and organize arts and cultural organizations. He also sings in a punk band and actively pursues career suicide every chance he gets.

Jannick Friis Christensen is Postdoctoral Researcher at Copenhagen Business School and Theme Lead for Gender and Sexuality in the CBS Diversity and Difference Business in Society Platform. Focusing on norm-critical approaches to organizing and researching diversity, Jannick has in recent years studied conventional work organizations from queer perspectives in collaboration with Danish labour unions. He also engages with alternative organizations, for example Roskilde Festival, where he explores the phenomenon of transgressive behavior, as well as practices for creating diverse and inclusive volunteer communities. His current project, financed by The Independent Research Fund Denmark, investigates the civil-religious public ritual of Copenhagen 2021 World Pride and its wider socially integrative potential through corporate collaboration.

Dide van Eck is a postdoctoral researcher in work and organization studies at the KU Leuven. Her research focuses on diversity management and organizational inclusion, particularly in service sector work contexts. She is interested in exploring how workplace diversity can be accommodated by more equal and inclusive forms of organizing.

Silvia Gherardi is Senior Professor of Sociology of Organization at the Department of Sociology and Social Research, University of Trento, Italy, where she founded the Research Unit on Communication, Organizational Learning, and Aesthetics (www.unitn.it/rucola). She is also Professor II at the School of Business, Society and Engineering, Mälardalens University, Sweden. She received the degree of "Doctor Honoris Causa" from Roskilde University (2005), East Finland University (2010) and St Andrews University (2014). Her research interests include feminist studies, entrepreneurship, epistemology of practice, and post-qualitative methodologies in organization studies.

Bontu Lucie Guschke is a PhD fellow in the Department of Organization at Copenhagen Business School. Her research centres on harassment and discrimination in contemporary organizational work settings. Empirically, she currently works with data from workplaces at Danish universities. Her focus lies within the research field of feminist and anti-racist organization studies, including perspectives from Black feminist and queer feminist theories. Bontu is part of Copenhagen Business School's Diversity and Difference Platform and in this context has worked on research projects in the area of gender and sexuality studies, including intersectional perspectives and norm-critical approaches to diversity work. As part of her engagement, Bontu consistently aims to work as a feminist killjoy.

Lindsay Hamilton is an organizational ethnographer with a particular interest in human-animal interactions at work and works as a senior lecturer at the University of York, UK. Her interdisciplinary research has focused upon slaughterhouses and meat-packing plants, farms, veterinary surgeries, shelters and zoos. She has co-authored several books in the field, including Animals at Work (Brill, 2013), Ethnography after humanism (Palgrave, 2017), and is the editor of *The Oxford Handbook of Animal Organization Studies* (Oxford University Press, forthcoming).

Veera Kinnunen holds a position of a senior lecturer in sociology at the University of Lapland, Finland. She is a sociologist and a cultural historian working on a threshold of more-than-human sociology, environmental humanities, and feminist ethics. Her research interests cover material culture of everyday life, and dwelling with more-than-human others such as microbes and waste. Throughout her research projects, she has been developing and experimenting with more-than-human ethnographic methodology. She is also currently working as a post-doctoral researcher in Envisioning Proximity tourism with New

Materialism funded by Academy of Finland. In her spare time, she experiments with her microbial companions; Bokashi composts and Kombucha jars, and dreams of a garden of her own.

Katrine Meldgaard Kjær is an Associate Professor at the IT University in Copenhagen. Her interests revolve around interdisciplinary and creative approaches to studying the intersection between the digital and health. She has previously published within organizational studies on ideas of fatness, disability and processes of in- and exclusion in relation to these.

Justine Grønbæk Pors is an Associate Professor at Copenhagen Business School. Justine's research explores new forms of organising, management and government and their adverse effects especially within the context of the welfare society. In her work, she strives to consider both broader policy developments and the professional practices and experiences in everyday organizational life. She is particularly interested in the contradictions and paradoxes inherent to contemporary policies and in subjectivity, affect and ghostly matters.

1 Introduction

Affect in Organization and Management

Carolyn Hunter and Nina Kivinen

Scholars of organizations are increasingly interested in everyday experiences through the study of embodiment and the lived body (see, e.g. Hancock and Tyler, 2009; Pullen and Rhodes, 2015; Fotaki and Daskalaki, 2021; Harding, Gilmore and Ford, 2021). Many have turned to the recent work on affect to understand the multiplicity of our identities at work, as employees, managers, co-workers and consumers are entangled with the world around us. Organizations may shape or move us, impacting upon our bodies and our sense of self (Shilling, 2012). When you walk into a workplace, you can gain a sense of this space of work, the people who work there and the artefacts and objects of that organization (Dale and Burrell, 2008). Entering a room, there are expectations and histories; multiple different ways of sensing the atmosphere of the room, the intensities between bodies and non-human objects. Take for example an organization with a 'fun' culture: those objects we encounter may encourage us to 'have fun', to tell jokes, to feel and demonstrate emotions such as happiness (Hunter, 2022). There may be expectations to experience organizational life in prescribed ways, although of course, the expected and the actual experience of employees may widely differ. To study the world of organizations, therefore, is to appreciate the connectedness with the world and to recognise the entanglements of the human, non-human and more-than-human in organizational life. It is this focus on affect being located in situated relationships with others, both human, non-human, and more-than human that this book explores.

Why affect, and what is it anyway?

Affect occurs in the encounters and relationships between objects and persons, where the encounter impacts and shapes bodies, surfaces and subjectivities. Affect is frequently introduced through a Spinozian perspective, where one is simultaneously affected and affecting (Massumi, 2015).

DOI: 10.4324/9781003182887-1

An example could be an encounter with an object strongly associated with a memory, where the touch, sight, smell or taste of the object may draw out sensations. Our favourite childhood food, the sound of sirens in the middle of the night, the colours of a painting, the smell of an old book. The body is both materially and socially constructed through these interactions, just as its presence constructs other meanings (Turner, 1992). Consider an illustrative example of an organizational encounter: a moment of conflict with another staff member while having a break in the staff kitchen. Even though employees ought to be positive and happy in this organization, and the kitchen is decorated to reflect this attitude, an argument occurs with raised voices. At that moment, the heart beats a little faster, and breathing increases. There is a tense atmosphere in the kitchen (Michels and Steyaert, 2017; Marsh and Śliwa, 2022). In this encounter, there is an entanglement of bodies, objects, feelings and atmosphere, and it is this moment of affect where decisions are made, politics are played out and identities like leader, manager and employees are enacted (Kenny, 2012).

Another way to understand affect is as an intensity, the sense of movement that occurs in an interaction. Intensities are embodied feelings, sensed through an impact that we may struggle to articulate or express (Seigworth and Gregg, 2010). Writers on affect may attempt to express the situated, relational and embodied through various methodologies including art-based methods, ethnographies or situated interviews (Kahl, 2020). Returning to the encounter in the kitchen, entering the space after the argument draws out a new but similar intensity: the sense of smell, sound and sight of the space bringing back a sense of tension. Affect also involves crossing a threshold, engaging with an object and memories associated with the object alters as an intensity is experienced (Massumi, 2015). The moment moves us, and then the intensity may drop or change, even though the moment of the argument has passed. It may still affect our future behaviour, for example, refraining from using the kitchen to avoid the person. As such, affect helps us understand the moment but also our understanding of the past and the future expectations of organizational life (see, e.g. Kenny and Fotaki, 2014, for an overview of affect at work from a psychosocial perspective, and Fotaki, Kenny and Vachhani, 2017, on how affect has in general been approached in management and organization studies).

Affect expands our understanding of organizations and work through the ways that moments shape our experiences, relationships and corporeality. Studying affect presents a shift to the emotive, unknowable and beyond-rational; however, it also asks us to question the very distinction between emotional and rational to recognise their entanglement

(Kahl, 2020). In the example of the conflict with a co-worker discussed earlier, affect is at once emotional, embodied and cognitive, all in the moment of the interaction. There is some debate about the difference between affect and emotion (see Chapter 2 on Sara Ahmed by Bontu Guschke, Jannick Christensen & Thomas Burø in this book), where affect involves a way of knowing and being part of the world. Those authors interested in emotions from this perspective, such as Sara Ahmed, argue that emotions do not derive just from an inner state, but instead are part of our engagement with the world around us. Other writers on affect focus more on our entanglement with the world and objects, such as Donna Haraway and Jane Bennett, asking us to recognise the importance of non-human objects and bodies in these relationships. Finally, writers on affect like Rosalyn Diprose also suggest that viewing the world as interconnected and inter-relational opens up new questions around how these relationships fix us into certain places or free us to see the world in different ways.

Affect focuses on our relations with the world around us, and of specific interest for this book, organizations. Organizations shape all types of encounters: they create expectations of how employees will feel, think, act, dress and speak. Organizations have a wide range of intended and unintended consequences for society and the environment. Reflecting a range of dimensions and perspectives on affect (Seigworth and Gregg, 2010), this book explores how subjects and agency are formed through their connections and entanglements with others, both human and the non- or more-than-human. To study affect, therefore, calls on researchers in management and organization studies to explore a range of 'bodies' in and around organizations. Non-human bodies, organizational spaces and objects can all play equally as important roles in affect as human bodies, a viewpoint that questions the anthropocentric tendencies of much of organizational scholarship.

Affect in management and organization studies

Affect has entered management and organization studies through some powerful papers published over the last few years (Vachhani, 2012; Kenny, 2012; Thanem and Wallenberg, 2015; Ashcraft, 2017; Fotaki, Kenny and Vachhani, 2017; Pullen, Rhodes and Thanem, 2017). These papers draw in particular on feminist thinking and for these authors affect enables the acknowledgement of a destabilized subject and the entanglement of the human, non-human and more-than-human, in particular drawing upon the work of thinkers such as Haraway and Bennett. Affect allows for a different subjectivity to emerge and through this an embodied and lived ethics (Dale and Latham, 2015). Since the publication of the first papers, a small but growing interest can be seen.

Within the field of organization and management affect is acknowledged as being political (Pullen, Rhodes and Thanem, 2017). Empirically affect has been studied in particular in the creative industries and the arts, politically offering different ways of inhabiting organizations (see, e.g. Bell and Vachhani, 2020; Hoedemaekers, 2018; Leclair, 2022; Michels and Steyaert, 2017). Affect allows for new ways to understand creativity and the creative process not as the work of an individual creative genius but as encounters that create unique and new constellations in the everyday which allows ideas to emerge. Affect has also provided new insights into studies of the dark sides of organizations, as well as resistance, where affect can be politically used to restrain, control and manage (see, e.g. Marsh and Śliwa, 2021; Vachhani and Pullen, 2019). For example, Ashcraft's (2017) critique of excellence and resistance in organization studies advocated for an inhabited criticism that acknowledges affective experience and presents an alternative posture of resistance. Here affect can help us understand the engagements of power, and the profound impact destructive organizational practices have on our understanding of self and others (see, e.g. van Amsterdam, van Eck and Meldgaard Kjær, 2022; Pouthier and Sondak, 2021). Affect works as a force to create collective solidarity and resistance, shifting the focus from individual experiences to affective solidarity through feminist activism (Vachhani and Pullen, 2019; also Baxter, 2021).

Most importantly perhaps, questions around affect have empowered researchers to rethink their practices of doing research and of academic writing (see, e.g. Gherardi, 2019; Otto and Strauß, 2019; Beyes and Steyaert, 2021). Affect encourages us to ask new questions, and to approach research in an embodied, ethical way that aims to capture ephemeral encounters and entanglements of human, non-human and more-than-human. For this, we need new practices that allow for affect to emerge. Writing differently is a crucial form of doing affect that allows for vulnerabilities to be visible, destabilising the writing subject and revealing the entanglement in which we are bound (see, e.g. Pullen, 2018; Kivinen, 2021) and as such stands against a masculine rationale that still prevails in academia.

Women writers on affect

Many of the women writers selected for this collection focus their writing on affect, with an interest to develop a specific area that addresses our understanding of lived experience and our connections to others, such as race, feminism, the everyday and ethics. Other writers in this collection tend to discuss affect as a background concept, as a conceptual tool within which they can explore embodiment, non-human objects and materiality. The chapters present new ways of discussing organizational life: Sara Ahmed, through emotions and race, Kathleen Stewart on affective moments and atmospheres, Jane Bennett on new materialism, Karen Barad on entanglement, Donna Haraway on more-than-human affect and Rosalyn Diprose on corporeal ethics. Feminism is a core feature of all their work, highlighting feminist writing with affective, connected and intersubjective possibilities. Focusing on publications by women writers on affect over the last 30 years, this book highlights ongoing debates about how organizations and work are constituted through everyday interactions which shape subjects, materials and the more-than-human.

We felt that a collection on women writers on affect was timely in this series, as affect offers a multiplicity of new perspectives and methodologies for researchers to explore, drawing on feminist critique and extending the discussion of affect as political. The debates discussed earlier often tie into other themes explored in the first five books in this series. The first connection is that of questioning our taken-for-granted normative approaches to studying organizations. This includes the work of writers like Hochschild (Ward, 2019), Höpfl (Karayiannis and Kostera, 2019), Douglas (Simpson and Hughes, 2020) and Irigaray (Vachhani, 2020), who question in various ways the view of organizations as neutral, depolitical and separate from emotion. This collection on affect also breaks down the binary of rationality and emotion through the analysis of affect as a way of knowing. The second theme which connects the series is an analysis of power. Examples of previous chapters include writing about activists such as the suffragette Garrud to explore embodied power (Kelly, 2019) and theorists such as bell hooks who challenge notions of power and race (Liu, 2019). Importantly, Haraway also raises critiques of ethnocentricisim in organization studies, through the assumptions of universality which benefit the powerful while ignoring 'others' (Prasad, Segarra and Villanueva, 2020). We return to the work of Haraway in this book to explore power relations between the 'more-than-human'. The series also opens up issues around ethics, where Butler (Harding, 2020) contributes towards understanding ethics as relationality and Berlant (Kenny, 2020) discusses cruel optimism as a way that affect becomes structured into inequality. We develop these themes by discussing how affects can empower and exclude, as well as provoke ethical questions of our interconnectedness with others. The third connection is that of feminism. An especially relevant connection is the writer Sedgwick (Taalas, 2019), who draws heavily on affect theory in her writing about queering and productive shame as a way to challenge normativity. This collection extends these debates on shame, queering and feminism through Ahmed's work on normativity in affective demands and also on queering writing as a form of writing differently (Taalas, 2019). This presents questions about how we can understand difference through experiences such as affect.

This collection on women writers on affect is the sixth book in the series and adds to the discussion in the other five texts in this series by understanding how power, gender and ethics present themselves through complex connections formed around workers and organizations. Critically it adds to the commentary on other women writers in organization studies at the level of everyday moments, understanding the contribution that relatively recent female writers on affect are having on management and organization studies. Following the aim of this series to explore and celebrate women writers, this book draws together different perspectives on affect as an emerging discussion. The writers selected for this collection make an important contribution to the field of affect: many of them were early thinkers whose use of affect inspired academics across not only the social sciences but also humanities and the sciences. In addition, many of them make profound insights related to feminist, queer, more-than-human and anti-racist approaches to the study of organizations.

The researchers and scholars who write in this collection are experts on affect and we are so grateful for their wonderful contributions. The collection opens with Bontu Guschke, Jannick Christensen & Thomas Burø's discussion of Sara Ahmed's work on affect. As the authors point out, Ahmed's work questions the very distinction between emotions and affects, and indeed is critical of how hierarchies emerged between emotions and affect. Ahmed asks what emotions 'do' or how we are affected by emotions in our interactions with others. Emotions are seen as sticky, in that, as affect is experienced and described through emotions, these emotions become connected to various people and objects. Bontu Guschke, Jannick Christensen & Thomas Burø draw out the importance of normativity in Ahmed's work, exploring how power relations in organization set up the expectation of emotions and affect. One of Ahmed's contributions is analysing societal patterns of privilege through affect, especially in the fields of feminist, anti-racist, and queer studies. Her work demonstrates how affects shape us, open up or close down possibilities to us and reproduce patterns of privilege through opportunities and disadvantages. Within organization studies, Ahmed's work has been critical of the study of whiteness, exclusion, diversity and difference and queering. The chapter concludes with a reflection of what her work could mean for academia in questioning normativity and providing new ways of thinking about resistance and activism.

In Chapter 3, Silvia Gherardi shifts the discussion of affect back to the personal, through a fictional conversation dreamt with Kathleen Stewart. Stewart's work introduces affect through an exploration of the every-day, played out in several observations of being in the world. The writing in this chapter intertwines affect as theory and affect as experience, using *collage* as an approach to writing differently, writing with the text as opposed to writing about it. Gherardi explores how affect through troubling the reader as they engage with the daydream as a performative text. In entering a conversation with Stewart's work, this explores affect in the relations between human and non-humans, as both material and also more than the physical characteristics. It also comments on affect within ethnographic work, as part of the daily rhythms of everyday life. In doing so, affect emerges as an important way in which we are shaped as subjects. In organization studies, exploring ordinary affects can open up powerful ways of understanding, or attunement to the qualities of organizational life, of being sensitive to fieldwork research and of writing about organizations.

Moving from the personal to the material, Lindsay Hamilton intro-duces Donna Haraway's writing on the 'more-than-human'. In her cyborg manifesto, Haraway sets out a radical approach to understand-ing human interactions with non-human machines and non-human animals. Enacting a feminist critique, her work presents a cyborg as a fictional hybrid of machine and organisms that form our social reality. Her later work has also been influential in critical animal studies and the decentring of the human subject. For organization studies, Haraway's work highlights in particular the complex relationships between peo-ple and technology and provides tools for understanding the agency of hybrid forms of working subjects (see also Prasad, Segarra and Villanueva, 2020 on the notion of passionate detachment). Lindsay Hamilton draws on Haraway's concept of blasphemy as category deviance to ask how we organise ourselves, animals and matter to privilege certain forms of knowledge. To open up other possibilities, Haraway returns to kinship as an alternative way to relate through the concept of 'becomings'. The affectual connections of kinship enable us to relate to others, human and non-human, in a form of non-optional reciprocity. For organizational scholars, realizing our connectedness, we can consider 'feeling' out these boundaries and connections to explore how they sustain different social relations, and where we may want to challenge or 'compost' them into new ways of relating.

Also drawing on our connections to the world around us, Jane Ben-nett's work is then considered by Justine Pors, who asks how affective states of wonder and enchantment can be explored through the vibrancy of matter. Justine Pors demonstrates how in Bennett's work everyday encounters can be experienced through an enchanting affect, where through our relationships with others and objects we are moved into a state which can hold both joy and pain, through rhythms and a sense of suspension. This being in the world focuses on our embodied presence which connects to materials and others, which are assembled into sometimes unexpected combinations. Bennett would describe this as a vibrant matter, or the ways in which materiality can be part of an assemblage that may move us. Folding back onto the previous chapters in this series, Bennett's work and other contributions to new materialism may offer a way for organization scholars to understand affect, embodiment and materiality, opening up questions around intersubjectivity and ethics of 'organised being'.

Chapter 6 also put into practice the concept of *writing differently*, entangling Karen Barad's theory on connectedness with the Noortje van Amsterdam, Katrine Kjaer and Dide van Eck's personal reflection on writing about and living through enacting affect theory. Human and non-human bodies and discourses come together in what Barad would refer to as inter-action: of entanglement of words, theory, emotions, animals, technology, objects and affects. In particular, the chapter draws out the importance of relationality in Barad's work, especially in relation to feminist community. Shifting between a personal and academic tone, the chapter explores what it means to be an academic writing on organizations. Through this, it extends what may be possible in our study of organizations and ethical responsibility that comes from 'always/already' being entangled. Organization in this chapter is not separate from the everyday but embedded in affect explored through travel, pets, academia, and sensations of shame.

Ethics draws together the work of many of the women writers in this collection, and as a result the final chapter in this collection focuses on how we can revisit our concept of ethics in organizations. Rosalyn Diprose's work, discussed in Chapter 7 by Veera Kinnunen, elaborates on this link, exploring how ethics can be formed through our interactions with others rather than as a universal moral code. Women writers explored in this series such as Ahmed, Bennett and Stewart argue that experiencing affect is important because it locates us within the world, connecting us to others, both human and non-human (see also the chapters on Barad and Haraway). Through these experiences, we can be unsettled, disrupted and become exposed to alternative ways of being. For example, Ahmed uses this principle to explore affect and race; Bennett to explore how wonder might shake us from predictable paths, and Stewart to elaborate on how everyday moments unsettle us. Diprose argues that this interconnectedness and unsettling affect open us to new experiences, and in doing so can present an opportunity for generosity towards those who are different to ourselves, which challenges many mainstream notions of business ethics and ethics in the workplace.

These chapters present not only an introduction to the six women writers on affect and their current impact on organizational studies but also the potential unmapped routes on affect theory which could be taken. Many of the chapters present thought-provoking potential directions to be explored. The need for new ideas and research is acute in organization studies, where viewing the world in different ways may help to address issues of global environmental crises, organizational ethics and inequality, fair treatment, and new ways to lead and manage organizations. Underpinned by feminism, the work of these women writers on affect brings a more inclusive view of how we can relate to others in a more than human world. Rather than being a definitive answer on 'what is affect' or what is important in the field, we hope that this collection acts to provoke new possibilities and ways of enacting organizations.

References

Ashcraft, K.L. (2017). "Submission" to the rule of excellence: Ordinary affect and precarious resistance in the labour of organization and management studies. *Organization*, 24(1), pp. 36–58.

Baxter, L.F. (2021). The importance of vibrant materialities in transforming affective dissonance into affective solidarity: How the Countess Ablaze organized the tits out collective. *Gender Work Organization*, 28, pp. 898–916.

Bell, E. and Vachhani, S.J. (2020). Relational encounters and vital materiality in the practice of craft work. *Organization Studies*, 41(5), pp. 681–701.

Beyes, T. and Steyaert, C. (2021). Unsettling bodies of knowledge: Walking as a pedagogy of affect. *Management Learning*, 52(2), pp. 224–242. https://doi.org/10.1177/1350507620979713

Dale, K. and Burrell, G. (2008). *The spaces of organisation & the organisation of space: Power, identity and materiality at work*. Basingstoke: Palgrave MacMillian.

Dale, K. and Latham, Y. (2015). Ethics and entangled embodiment: Bodies – materialities – organization, *Organization*, 22(2), pp. 166–182.

Fotaki, M., and Daskalaki, M. (2021). Politicizing the body in the anti-mining protest in Greece. *Organization Studies*, 42(8), pp. 1265–1290.

Fotaki, M., Kenny, K. and Vachhani, S.J. (2017). Thinking critically about affect in organization studies: Why it matters. *Organization*, 24(1), pp. 3–17.

Gherardi, S. (2019). Theorizing affective ethnography for organization studies. *Organization*, 26(6), pp. 741–760.

Hancock, P. and Tyler, M. (2009). *The management of everyday life*. Basingstoke: Palgrave MacMillian.

Harding, N. (2020). Judith Butler: Theorist and political activist. In: *Morality, ethics and responsibility in organization and management*. Abingdon: Routledge, pp. 73–89.

Harding, N., Gilmore, S. and Ford, J. (2021). Matter that embodies: Agentive flesh and working bodies/selves. *Organization Studies*. Online first. https://doi.org/10.1177/0170840621993235

Hoedemaekers, C. (2018). Creative work and affect: Social, political and fantasmatic dynamics in the labour of musicians. *Human Relations*, 71(10), pp. 1348–1370.

Hunter, C. (2022). Happy objects at work: The circulation of happiness. *Culture and Organization*, 28(2), pp. 129–147.

Kahl, A. (2020). *Analyzing affective societies: Methods and methodologies*. Abingdon: Routledge.

Karayiannis, A. and Kostera, M. (2019). The inspirations of Heather Höpfl: Taking heart from radical humanism. In: *Beyond rationality in organization and management*. Abingdon: Routledge, pp. 54–72.

Kelly, S. (2019). Edith Garrud: The jujutsuffragette. In: *Power, politics and exclusion in organization and management*. Abingdon: Routledge, pp. 8–23.

Kenny, K. (2012). 'Someone big and important': Identification and affect in an international development organization. *Organization Studies*, 33(9), pp. 1175–1193.

Kenny, K. (2020). Lauren Berlant: Cruel organizations. In: *Morality, ethics and responsibility in organization and management*. Abingdon: Routledge, pp. 56–72.

Kenny, K. and Fotaki, M., eds. (2014). *The psychosocial and organization studies: Affect at work (studies in the psychosocial)*. London: Palgrave Macmillan.

Kivinen, N. (2021). Writing grief, breathing hope. *Gender Work Organization*, 28, pp. 497–505.

Leclair, M. (2022). The atmospherics of creativity: Affective and spatial materiality in a designer's studio. *Organization Studies*. Online first. https://doi.org/10.1177/01708406221080141

Liu, H. (2019). Decolonising organizations with bell hooks. In: *Power, politics and exclusion in organization and management*. Abingdon: Routledge, pp. 83–98.

Marsh, D. and Śliwa, M. (2022). Making a difference through atmospheres: The orange alternative, laughter and the possibilities of affective resistance. *Organization Studies*, 43(4), pp. 477–496.

Massumi, B. (2015). *Politics of affect*. Cambridge: Polity Press.

Michels, C. and Steyaert, C. (2017). By accident and by design: Composing affective atmospheres in an urban art intervention. *Organization*, 24(1), pp. 79–104.

Otto, B.D. and Strauß, A. (2019). The novel as affective site: Uncertain work as impasse in wait until spring, Bandini. *Organization Studies*, 40(12), pp. 1805–1822.

Pouthier, V. and Sondak, H. (2021). When shame meets love: Affective pathways to freedom from injurious bodily norms in the workplace. *Organization Studies*, 42(3), pp. 385–406.

Prasad, A., Segarra, P. and Villanueva, C.E. (2020). Situating knowledges through feminist objectivity in organization studies: Donna Haraway and the partial perspective. In: *Rethinking culture, organization and management*. Abingdon: Routledge, pp. 73–88.

Pullen, A. (2018). Writing as labiaplasty. *Organization*, 25(1), pp. 123–130.

Pullen, A. and Rhodes, C. (2015). Ethics, embodiment and organizations. *Organization*, 22(2), pp. 159–165.

Pullen, A., Rhodes, C. and Thanem, T. (2017). Affective politics in gendered organizations: Affirmative notes on becoming-woman. *Organization*, 24(1), pp. 105–123.

Seigworth, G. and Gregg, M. (2010). An inventory of shimmers. In: M. Gregg and G. Seigworth, eds., *The affect theory reader*. Durham: Duke University Press.

Shilling, C. (2012). *The body and social theory*. London: Sage Publications.

Simpson, R. and Hughes, J. (2020). Mary Douglas: The cultural and material manifestations of dirt and dirty work. In: *Rethinking culture, organization and management*. Abingdon: Routledge, pp. 25–38.

Taalas, S.L. (2019). Witnessing eve: Eve Kosofsky Sedgwick. In: *Gender, embodiment and fluidity in organization and management*. Abingdon: Routledge, pp. 75–91.

Thanem, T. and Wallenberg, L. (2015). What can bodies do? Reading Spinoza for an affective ethics of organizational life. *Organization*, 22(2), pp. 235–250.

Turner, B.S. (1992). *Regulating bodies: Essays in medical sociology*. London: Routledge.

Vachhani, S.J. (2012). (Re)creating objects from the past – affect, tactility and everyday creativity. *Management and Organizational History*, 8(1), pp. 91–104.

Vachhani, S.J. (2020). Luce Irigaray's philosophy of the feminine: Exploring a culture of sexual difference in the study of organizations. In: *Rethinking culture, organization and management*. Abingdon: Routledge, pp. 55–72.

Vachhani, S.J. and Pullen, A. (2019). Ethics, politics and feminist organizing: Writing feminist infrapolitics and affective solidarity into everyday sexism. *Human Relations*, 72(1), pp. 23–47.

van Amsterdam, N., van Eck, D. and Meldgaard Kjær, K. (2022). On (not) fitting in: Fat embodiment, affect and organizational materials as differentiating agents. *Organization Studies*. Online first. https://doi.org/10.1177/01708406221074162.

Ward, J. (2019). Arlie Russell Hochschild. In: *Beyond rationality in organization and management*. Abingdon: Routledge, pp. 22–36.

2 Sara Ahmed

A Return to Emotions

Bontu Lucie Guschke, Jannick Friis Christensen and Thomas Burø

Introduction, or "There are happy babies all over my , Instagram feed"

Imagine you have a friend who wants a happy baby. Eventually, your friend manages to have a baby, presumably a happy one. You have seen countless pictures of her happy baby on Instagram. When you meet your friend, her baby is crying in the stroller. Your friend says, "He is not usually like this. Usually he is happy." She comments on his being unhappy: "He is out of character." According to Sara Ahmed, who uses the happy baby example in *Willful Parts: Problem Characters or the Problem of Characters* (2011), this raises at least three problems. First, what does it mean to *be* happy? Second, what does it mean that the baby is *usually* happy? Third, what does it mean to be *out of character*? We start this chapter, in which we introduce some of Ahmed's work, by exploring these questions, which we consider to be heuristic in illuminating her contribution to affect and organization. We examine some of her main concepts, specifically will and willfulness, as well as those of affect community, mood and moodwork, attunement, and alignment. Functioning as a conceptual basis, they allow us to answer the aforementioned questions by explaining how happiness works as a demand. Moreover, unpacking these concepts enables us to identify their precursors by presenting the conceptual influences that have inspired Ahmed's work.

The remainder of the chapter dives deeper into Ahmed's conceptualizations around affect and emotion, putting forth two main points. We present Ahmed's conception of "diversity work as moodwork" to illustrate how emotions circulate in organizations. This illustration allows us to highlight how her scholarship links emotion with normativity, which, in turn, makes it possible to investigate affect in relation to organizational norms and power structures. Further, we suggest that her work can be understood as a (re)turn to emotion rather than part of an affective turn

DOI: 10.4324/9781003182887-2

per se, as, according to Ahmed (2014b, p. 208), emotion and affect are inextricably linked: "Emotions, in other words, involve bodily processes of affecting and being affected, or to use my own terms, emotions are a matter of how we come into contact with objects and others." In the way we structure the chapter – working our way through the different concepts she develops in relation to emotions and affect rather than starting with one clear definition or conceptualization – we aim to do justice to Ahmed's focus on how emotions circulate socially: what they *do* more than what they *are* (Gorton, 2007). Finally, we introduce a few recent examples of how Ahmed's work has been taken up and put to use by organization scholars, before ending the chapter with our own reflections on where (else) Ahmed's authorship may take us.

Happy people are good people – happiness as a demand

Ahmed claims that happiness is a normative state of being (Ahmed, 2011). To *be* happy is a *demand*. Happiness is something everyone, babies included, ought to be and try to become if they happen not to be happy. Happiness is thus considered a state of being that one can choose, an act of volition. It is, moreover, a state of being that one is expected to inhabit commonly; *usually* one ought to be happy. Ahmed's conception of happiness as a state of being to which one can set one's mind is coupled with the concept of *the willful subject*. Conceptually, "will" relates both to the individual person's ability to be someone who wills – or, more precisely, who is *willing* to want – what one ought to will and want, and to the individual who is strong or stubborn enough to will otherwise, thus *willful* (Ahmed, 2014c, p. 133). Willingness is the product of subjectification, the processes through which someone (a baby) becomes an individual person (this baby) equipped with ideas, practices, standards, norms, and a relation to self. We learn to will certain objects that are desirable – such as good looks, a big house, decent pay – and, at the same time, we learn to think for ourselves. "Character" is the ascribed property of a person who wills as everybody (the imagined norm) wills, that is, someone who has used their faculty for volition to direct their orientation towards what they are expected to will – in this case, happiness. To be out of character, then, simply means that one does not will what everybody wills.

Happiness functions as a penultimate positive feeling. It is emblematic of the good life, and it is difficult to imagine that it is not worth striving for. Why would anyone not choose at least to try to be happy? If someone told you that they wanted to be happy, it would, nowadays, be seen as odd if you asked to know why or to doubt their ambition. Etymologically, "happy" is an adjective constructed from "hap," which means "chance." In earlier times "happy" meant "good fortune" – and not only in English. The same holds true across many other languages, including German, in which the word for happy (*glücklich*) relates to *Glück*, which means "luck." The Danish *lykke* comes from the Low German *lucke* and *gelucke*, referring to fate and, literally, one's lot (*lod* in Danish) in life. In pre-modernity, therefore, happiness is a chance operation (Brinkmann, 2020). It happens. Happiness is the emotional state of being of those who are, fortunately, smiled upon by fate. But in neoliberal postmodernity, happiness is not considered random or a result of good fortune; it is seen as a choice, a matter of will (Ahmed, 2009, p. 2, 2010b, p. 29/ch.1). The idea is that if you work hard enough, anything can be made to happen; consequently, if you put in the labour, you can even conquer your own happiness. Happy becomes another word for "successful" and "successful" another word for "good." Happy people, it seems, are good people. The notable point is that when we think of happiness as a norm, we are invited to ask: What happens when you are not happy, and how is happiness enforced?

Affect community, mood, attunement and alignment

There is a general point to take away from the example of happiness as a normative state of being. Ahmed claims that happiness is not the only demanded emotion, as any given emotion can become normative insofar as a context, such as an organization, requires that its members attune their being to align with certain emotions (Ahmed, 2014a, 2014b). That some emotions are more contextually proper than others is perhaps well known to most people who have worked in an organized setting; with Ahmed, we can claim that part of an organizational structure is the emotional architecture, those states of being that dominate and are promoted as desirable. Some organizations are even defined by their emotions. The UK parliament, for example, would not be the same without MPs loudly expressing their immediate feelings about each other's speeches. Soldiers would be of little use for warfare if they did not learn how to hate (or at the very least not love) their enemies. And even "rational" algorithms used for trading at the world's stock exchanges may behave like "hysterical bitches" (Borch, 2020). Generally, if we examine any organization critically, we will most likely find that part of its informal power relations, if not part of its formal structure, is a set of emotions that organizational members are supposed to embody and express.

To conceptualize how the normativity of emotions – and, in particular, the happiness demand – functions, Ahmed offers four interrelated concepts: *affect community*, *mood*, *attunement*, and *alignment*. Imagine an organizational context in which a certain set of emotions is considered to be the norm. For simplicity and for the sake of argument, we will stick with happiness. Group members connect and relate to each other through a shared affective state of being happy, and the community expresses itself in the form of a collective happy mood. As we become part of an affect community, we share its happy mood; we "get caught up in feelings that are not our own . . . [m]oods become almost like companions" (Ahmed, 2014a, p. 15). We attune to the mood of the community; we adjust our affective state of being to align with the community's normative affects. Attunement is a concept for thinking how, at the level of being, we come to resonate with the general mood of the affect community. At the same time, attunement describes a requirement for community membership. For you to pass as part of a community – or organizational member – your manner of being affected has to be aligned with the right way of being affected. Aligning in the right way, "not only as being with, but being with in a similar way" (Ahmed, 2014a, p. 16), requires affective labour (see also Hochschild, 1983).

Performing affective labour, or moodwork, is demanded especially of those who are deemed as late arrivals to the scene. Think of the new organizational member, still a stranger, who is meant to integrate into the workplace. They are expected to align with the general happy mood. If they are unhappy, they are not attuned. Being estranged from happiness renders them a stranger (Ahmed, 2021). Affectively non-aligned individuals, such as the sulky or sombre musician in the orchestra at your big happy wedding, stand out. To be "in the mood" is a requirement for fitting in and passing as a member. Ahmed suggests that a shared mood functions as an "affective lens" that makes the world appear to us and affect us in certain ways (Ahmed, 2014a, p. 14). To illustrate this point, think of a married same-sex couple at the big happy *heterosexual* wedding, spoiling the "good" mood (Ahmed, 2008b, p. 6) and being seen as troublemakers when alienated by the neat male-female seating arrangement (see, e.g. Basner et al., 2018). Affect in this case is not an empirical object as much as a matter of investigating the actions that emotions perform, including what effects follow from them (Ahmed, 2004). Breaking with the shared "affective lens" threatens the ability to be part of and easily becomes an enforcement mechanism for aligning to, the affect community.

Conceptual lineages

Ahmed's conceptual landscape is inhabited by a multiplicity of intersecting philosophical lineages. To begin with, the Dutch seventeenth-century philosopher Baruch Spinoza was the first to describe the concept of affect in the sense used by many contemporary scholars. To Spinoza, the world is made up of bodies. Spinoza's body is more than a human body; it may be an idea, a weather phenomenon, a poison. Any such body has the capacity to affect or be affected by other bodies (Spinoza, 2006, pp. 3–4), the point being that to be affected means to be changed somehow. This sense is retained in the idea that emotions change us, but, to Spinoza, affect transcends emotions. Bodies often need the affect of other bodies to be able to function (we need only think of coffee!). This simple conceptualization has profound implications because it leads to an ontology in which bodies are contingent upon their affective relations with other bodies. For Ahmed, the bodily ability to be touched physically and emotionally is "that which makes it possible to be for others" (Ahmed, 2002, p. 563). Even the boundaries between bodies exist only through being traversed and contested when one body affects the other (Ahmed, 2000, p. 49). This ontology of bodies being (for others) through their affective relations, for example, becomes visible in Ahmed's conception of "the stranger," a body that becomes othered "through the relations of touch between bodies recognizable as friendly or [in this case] strange" (Ahmed, 2000, p. 49).

The second conceptual influence comes from the phenomenology of Edmund Husserl, for whom consciousness is always intentional (Husserl, 1970). The mind is always orientated towards something in the world that it perceives through its senses, as some objects move to the perceptual foreground and into proximity while others are pushed to the background or left out. This approach enables an analysis of how a life world customarily *orientates* consciousness towards certain objects. Ahmed uses *orientation* in relation to affect to describe how bodies inhabit and extend into space. How we are orientated in the world implicates which objects we turn toward, which bodies we face, and hence how we are touched (Ahmed, 2006b). We are touched by what comes near us; in other words, by enabling touchability, proximity allows us to be affected. Think again of "the stranger"; the body that is othered remains distant, while those recognized as friendly are those we turn toward. It is, then, easier to be touched by the fate of a "friendly" colleague than the suffering of a "stranger." Following Husserl, Martin Heidegger developed a phenomenology of being, conceiving being as *attuned* to different modes (e.g. dwelling, working) and analysing the being of bodies according to how they appear to humans (e.g. the hammer as a tool) (Heidegger, 1970/1927). In other words, being is always being *as* something. No one simply is. We see this influence in how Ahmed derives her understanding of, for example, mood or attunement from Heidegger's "*Stimmung*" as being in relation to others (Ahmed, 2014a).

Postcolonial theory, insofar as it is one theoretical standpoint, is an important source of ideas informing Sara Ahmed's work. Most important is the concept of the "subaltern other," the colonial subject. To understand and conceive what it means to be a person in a colonial situation requires attention to the myriad ways in which the situation "tells" the colonized person of their status as a colonized subject. Fanon – a scholar whose work Ahmed has "travelled with . . . for many years" (Ahmed, 2021, p. 15) – inquired how a person with "black skin" desires and learns to wear a "white mask" (Fanon, 2008) and, in the process, created the prototypical concept for colonial subjectification: the process through which a person suffering colonization becomes an "other" to the colonizer, no matter the degree to which they succeed in emulating the colonizer's morals and values. To provide an example to which we shall return at the end of the chapter, we see this influence in what Ahmed terms a "phenomenology of whiteness," in which whiteness "becomes [a] social and bodily orientation given that some bodies will be more at home in a world that is orientated around whiteness" (Ahmed, 2007, p. 160). A double line of inquiry thus runs through postcolonial theory since, to understand who and what the other is, one also needs to understand to whom and what they are imagined to be other. By exploring the concept of the Third World woman, we learn a great deal about how so-called "first world" women imagine themselves: as different from those women in Third World countries who are "religious," "oppressed," "revolutionary," and so on (Mohanty, 1988).

At the core of this conceptual work lies a troubling epistemological dilemma. On the one hand, it requires an anti-essentialist stance to oppose the colonial knowledge system that determines the essential nature of the subaltern (e.g. "the African is lazy," "the Arab is cunning") as an integral part of the system of colonial domination and occupation. On the other hand, it recognizes the political utility of strategic essentialism (we, the women, the native) as a foundation for solidarity and struggle for rights and self-determination (Spivak, 1985). In other words, invoking a collective identity always involves aligning the political struggle with the system of colonial power-knowledge, which works by fixing identity to render it "other." Ahmed works with a variety of different figures, such as the feminist killjoy, the unhappy queer, the melancholic migrant, and the angry black women (e.g. Ahmed, 2010b), who bridge this tension. She describes how they become "affect aliens" as they are deemed "other," affectively unaligned, while simultaneously using them to herald their "political potential and energy" (Ahmed, 2014a, p. 224) in resisting domination.

Finally, a certain line of inquiry in feminist epistemology is a necessary condition for Ahmed's work (Ahmed, 1996). Here, the traditional form of the epistemological question "what can we know, and how do we know what we know?" is replaced with "how and what do we know *as women*?" Part of the feminist struggle has been to render legitimate knowledges that deviate from a dominant male norm, politically as well as scientifically. At the risk of reduction, then, feminist epistemology asks what kind of knowledge claims women can produce, given their situation, and inevitably troubles the idea that epistemology and knowledge are gender neutral. Ahmed (2017) refers to her Pakistani aunt, Gulzar Bano, as her first feminist inspiration. It is important to mention this because it matters from whom and where we find or get our feminism. In Ahmed's (2017, p. 4) own words, "It is important that I learned this feminist lesson from my auntie in Lahore, Pakistan, a Muslim woman, a Muslim feminist, a brown woman. It might be assumed that feminism travels from West to East. . . . That is not my story. . . . Feminism travelled to me, growing up in the West, from the East." While we have highlighted four different conceptual lineages that are central to the apparatus that Ahmed has developed, we hope the reader can appreciate that her sources are multiple. There are, of course, other points of inspiration, for example queer studies (Ahmed, 2006b, 2019), which should remind us that her position is not easily reduced to being just that of phenomenology, philosophy, postcolonialism, or feminism. Nor should it be.

Emotions and affect

Ahmed's work has contributed substantially to a scholarly understanding of affect and the development of affect theory. Interestingly, however, Ahmed frequently uses emotions to refer to what is commonly understood as affect. For her, emotions are inseparable from bodily sensations (Ahmed, 2014b). While much of her work is orientated towards text. Her scholarship is ripe with metaphors and (linguistic) figures, through which text, according to her, performs different emotions and becomes thick with affect. Thus, emotion is not to be found in text per se, but as an effect of the naming of emotion. A recurring metaphor in Ahmed's authorship is the "brick wall" (e.g. Ahmed, 2006a, 2012, 2017, 2019). She makes use of the brick wall metaphor, for instance, to describe how diversity work is emotional work: You get tired, frustrated, if not depressed, from "banging your head against a brick wall" (Ahmed, 2017, p. 135), which is what institutional resistance to diversity and change feels like. For that reason, she often also refers to her metaphorical wall as "institutional," by which she means that it appears only to those who are misaligned or out of tune simply because of how they are in the world. If, for example, heterosexuality is the solidified mode of being and doing, to inhabit that world as heterosexual would be to go with the flow, whereas if one is not heterosexual and thus differently orientated, the "flow acquires the density of a thing, something solid" (Ahmed, 2017, p. 146). The flow does not feel "flowy" anymore but like an obstacle that requires active resistance. The materialization of the symbolic wall therefore renders real the way in which some bodies become out of place and, as a possible result, disorient others (Ahmed, 2006b).

Ahmed subscribes to a dual definition of diversity work as both the work of changing existing institutions *and* the work done by nonconforming bodies to "fit in" or not stick out, to be less out of tune (Ahmed, 2017, p. 135). Here, emotion clearly connects to affect: Diversity work is a matter of navigating affective atmospheres of, for example, racially charged interactions, sexist encounters, or homophobic abuse. Diversity work is moodwork. Here, we see connections to the scholarship of Hochschild (1983), specifically the notion of emotional labour as the work of aligning one's feelings (or the expression thereof) to meet the emotional requirements of an organization. Ahmed would say that the emotional labour of closing the gap between how you feel and how you should feel operates as a form of "feeling fetishism" (Ahmed, 2014b, p. 149), since the comfort of those who already feel at home depends on the work of others (diversity subjects) to minimize the discrepancy between how they might actually be feeling and how they ought to, thereby downplaying their difference or otherness. Perhaps for that reason, she appears to be especially fond of the "feminist killjoy" and its variant, the angry Black woman (explored by Lorde, 1984; hooks, 2000) killing feminist joy, as moody figures (e.g. Ahmed, 2010a, 2014b, 2017, 2019) – moody because they are not attuned and might even deliberately get in the way of attunement (Ahmed, 2014a). To be willing to become a killjoy, then, is "to be willing to get in the way of any happiness that does not have your agreement" (Ahmed, 2014b, p. 225). The killjoy figure, however, is also illustrative of how one may become alienated affectively, not necessarily because one wills it, but because one affects others the wrong way. One becomes an "affect alien," for example, if not happily affected by an object (say, the unhappy, usually happy baby) that supposedly should make one happy, or if one is unable to feel happy on the day of one's own wedding (supposedly the happiest day of one's life). This failure to feel happy is taken by others as sabotaging their happiness too, in which case one inadvertently becomes a killjoy (Ahmed, 2010a).

Because a killjoy is someone who wills other than what one ought to will, we may think of the killjoy figure as one of Ahmed's willful subjects.

As outlined, the concepts of *will* and *willfulness* play a vital role in her conceptualization of affect and emotions, since they explain how emotions can get anchored upon a normative foundation. Social and organizational norms become social goods, for instance, through the promise of happiness. This mechanism leads to the condition that a subject who is *willing* to follow the general will does *not* become a willful subject but a good and happy subject. In other words, what is willed for you is considered good, whereas your own willfulness against such a norm is seen as bad or even dangerous. Willful subjects, such as the feminist killjoy, are those who resist the general will, resist an orientation towards happiness; "To claim *to be* willful or to describe oneself or one's stance *as* willful is to claim the very word that has historically been used as a technique for dismissal" (Ahmed, 2014c, p. 133).

The affective turn as a (re)turn to emotion

Both the brick wall and feminist killjoy say something about how Ahmed conceptualizes emotion in relation to affective intensity. Her analytical focus is not on what emotions *are* per se, but how they circulate socially and what emotions *do* (Gorton, 2007). In the seminal work *The Cultural Politics of Emotion* (first published in 2004), Ahmed (2014b) examines the circulation of the objects that emotions are directed towards and how different emotions involve different orientations towards those objects. In brief, we may sense we share the same emotion, but that does not mean we have the same relationship to a given object. Orientation towards something means that, when affected by the object, we may move towards or away from it, thereby establishing a relation of either proximity or distance – as for example with the attachment in the feeling of love for the familiar (family, fellow-Christian) or the detachment of fearing the stranger (the other, refugees). Simply put, merely to think of a given object can bring up certain emotions, and vice versa, because objects become "sticky" in the sense that they accumulate affective value, which is another way of saying that they, the objects, maintain certain associations over time (Ahmed, 2021).

Importantly, however, it cannot be deduced from this that a feeling resides in an object or a body, even though it might be ascribed to one. Nor is a feeling "just there" in a room. As Ahmed writes, objects and bodies might "become sticky, saturated with affects," but only by being "understood retrospectively as the cause of feeling" (2008b, pp. 3–4), a causality which, according to her, we must rethink. Instead, feelings are an effect of our orientation. Different orientations towards objects implicate different emotions by being affected differently. "To be affected 'in a good way' thus involves an orientation towards something as being good" (Ahmed, 2008b, p. 4). Happiness, for instance, becomes an orientation towards objects that are supposed to make you happy: a wedding, a baby. It becomes a promise: something that results from following a social norm of orientating oneself in "the right way." In contrast, think back to the position of the affect alien. She might be the one who "refuses to share an orientation toward certain things as being good, because she does not find the objects that promise happiness to be quite so promising" (Ahmed, 2008b, p. 6).

In summary, we may say that emotions are inseparable from the dual capacity to affect and to be affected, and they are therefore a matter of "how we come into contact with objects and others" (Ahmed, 2014b, p. 208). Rather than as a turn to affect, it is therefore more fitting to treat Ahmed's work as a *re*-turn to emotion (Ahmed, 2014b, p. 209). This claim brings to the fore a potential implication of the affective turn: that it creates a distinction between affect and emotion, privileging the former over the latter (Ahmed, 2008a). To assume their separation, and then claim novelty in a turn towards affect, is to imply a problematic mind–body dichotomy, which we avoid if affect and emotion are understood as mutually implicated (Ahmed, 2014b, p. 206).

Ahmed, affect and organization

Refocusing on organization studies, we can continue our line of questioning by asking what Ahmed's conceptual work in relation to affect allows us to do to/with organizations. This question is perhaps best explored by examining how Ahmed's work has been taken up by researchers in the field of organization studies. What kind of questions have her concepts prompted us to pose? What knowledge claims become possible by working and thinking with her concepts? We are, for obvious reasons, unable to provide an exhaustive overview of Ahmed's reception within organization studies. Instead, we outline five recent examples that we believe show how her work has opened new theoretical as well as empirical avenues in this research area. Affect is not necessarily the primary analytical category in all five examples, but affect (and emotion) can – as we will show – be teased out in their relationship with other categories (Schmitz and Ahmed, 2014), an effect we have achieved with the categories of will and happiness. We conclude by suggesting an additional contribution of Ahmed's scholarship: that it invites, or even demands, us to question our own orientations, attunements and affective commitments.

Christensen, Muhr and Just (2020) use Ahmed's phenomenology of whiteness as an ongoing history that orientates bodies in specific directions, affecting how the bodies (can) take up space (Ahmed, 2007) or, in the case of this study, voice their opinion. The authors use this particular part of Ahmed's authorship to analyse how racialized (and also white) opinion leaders are organized in Danish public debate to be orientated around whiteness as an unseen backdrop. Consequently, opinion leaders whose bodies merge into this backdrop do not have to face their whiteness, meaning they are not oriented towards it. The opposite is true for opinion leaders in non-white bodies; they become noticeable as deviant from the constructed norm of whiteness. As such, they are positioned to speak from a minority point of view but with "white voice," a way of speaking that is recognizable to the majority, and often also ending up representing racialized subjects as a group. An alternative effect of whiteness that can be observed in the study, however, is the outright silencing of racialized subjects by majority voices that speak on their behalf. It is Ahmed's work that enables the analytical sensitivity for understanding how whiteness "functions as a form of public comfort by allowing bodies to extend into spaces that have already taken their shape" (Ahmed, 2007, p. 158) – white bodies, that is.

Another piece that focuses on the functioning of whiteness in organizations is an article by Dar and Ibrahim (2019), which conceptualizes the production of shame as a mechanism of "White governmentality" over the "Blackened body" in UK academia. The authors argue that producing shame in the Blackened body is a tool to silence, alienate and degrade women of colour. It works to both dispossess and discipline them, as it leads to women of colour understanding themselves as "lacking," for instance, networks, motivation and likeability: "Generating shame in her and making her co-produce it so that she also owns it (through her deteriorating self-image) serves to shift the gross levels of lack in the institution towards residing in her flesh" (Dar and Ibrahim, 2019, p. 1248). At the same time, it reaffirms whiteness as a norm that legitimizes the exclusion of women of colour from the academy. Drawing on Ahmed's (2014b) work on the sociality of emotion, the authors analyse how emotions – here, shame – shape and modify what bodies can do, conceptualizing the production of shame as a form of affective management. On this basis, they urge organizational scholars to pay closer attention to this "affective regime to tame, discipline and eke compliance from the Blackened body" (Dar and Ibrahim, 2019, p. 1243).

Ahmed's work has exercised significant influence upon critical scholarship on diversity and difference in organizations. Tyler (2019, p. 54) draws upon Ahmed's conceptualization of *the stranger* to emphasize that it is "the mode of encounter with the Other rather than the latter's ontological status that can open up the possibility of recognizing rather than containing or assimilating the Other's difference." Tyler (2019, p. 54) uses this to argue that critical diversity scholars investigating organizational practices need to inquire "not how difference can be made to fit into an organizational norm, but rather how difference has the potential to rupture the normative conditions and corporate imperatives governing its organization." By showing how the Other is created through affective processes of inclusion and exclusion, Ahmed encourages diversity scholars to relate difference to potentiality for norm-transgression rather than to something to be contained, thereby offering another critical contribution to the field of organizational scholarship. As another example, while not a central concept in Christensen's (2021) study of alternative organization within the context of Denmark's Roskilde Festival, affect here works as a conceptual *tool*, enabling Christensen to analyse an LGBT+ community's staging of a spontaneous pride parade in the festival's camping area as a "queer use" (Ahmed, 2019) of the festival space. The parade "released potential by putting the camping sites to a use different from what was intended" (Christensen, 2021, p. 165), the point being that this particular use of the camping area is queer only because the festival space is not, and the affect of being othered and feeling alien brings this to the fore.

Ahmed's influence on queer(ing) organization studies becomes most visible in her suggestion of a queer phenomenology (Ahmed, 2006c). Vitry (2020) mobilizes this suggestion by exploring the queering of bodies, spaces, and organizing in capitalist as well as alternative modes of organizing. Investigating the norms that persist in organizational spaces, Vitry not only reveals their straightening effects and how they make non-conforming bodies feel out of place; she also proposes strategies of resistance based upon "queerer forms of organizing" (*ibid.*, 12). Ahmed's (2006b) *Queer Phenomenology* provided "a useful theoretical tool to examine the ways capitalist and other normative spaces queer bodies" (Vitry, 2020, p. 12) and enabled the critical reading of "including" queered subjects as another extension of heteronormativity. A core contribution of Ahmed's work thus lies in providing a focal avenue for organization studies to explore and conceptualize queer(ing) practices from an affective perspective. That is to say, more broadly, that it allows for critical engagement with the norms permeating organizational settings. Such critical engagement has been linked to organizational heteronormativity as much as to norms of whiteness in organizations, highlighting once more Ahmed's contributions in the fields of feminist, anti-racist, and queer studies, and the potential of linking insights from these fields to research in organizational studies through her work.

Future orientations

As a final comment, we wish to suggest that Ahmed's work challenges each of us working in the organization field – and, in a broader sense, in the organizational contexts of the academy – to think about our own affective commitments. We need to question to which affect communities we belong and to whom we are attuned. What moodwork do we engage in to create affective alignment? What does the general will orientate us towards and who becomes willful by orientating themselves differently? We might come to recognize and criticize who becomes an affect alien in our organizational settings and how to react if someone disrupts the "good" mood.

As Bell and de Gama (2018) suggest in their reflection on the responsibilities of critical scholars, particularly in "uncritical" (Willmott, 2013) academic organizations, academic scholarship as well as organizational membership cannot be separated from ethical or political concerns. Reflecting on the possibility of "critical futures," they propose a critical practice that "involves feeling for yourself and for others, taking accountability for one's actions, and being aware of one's own positionality" (Bell and de Gama, 2018, p. 943). Becoming aware of one's own positionality might be rephrased to inquiring and questioning one's own orientation. What bodies are we oriented towards within the organizational context of academic work and with whom does this bring us into proximity? Ahmed's work leaves no doubt that an orientation towards whiteness as the norm in academia – seen, for instance, in the fact that "our curricula almost exclusively teach the opinions of white American and European men" (Dar et al., 2020) – influences not only the knowledge we accept as legitimate but the bodies we encounter and the lives we acknowledge as valuable. As we have outlined, our orientation implicates our way of inhabiting and extending into space, thus bringing certain objects and bodies into proximity. Our orientation might thus inhibit our ability of "feeling for others," or at least position some others outside the realm of bodies we can touch and be touched by (i.e. have the capacity to affect and to be affected by us). To be more specific, a lack of Black and brown bodies and knowledges in the academy might come to affect our ability to feel for anyone who is "other" to a white, male norm of being and knowing.

How, then, can we also feel for those "other others"? Ashcraft (2017, p. 44) proposes the notion of "inhabited criticism" in the form of "ordinary resistances," "micropractices," or "microemancipation" through "mundane, covert, informal and emergent, individual and interactional, localized and fleeting practices such as cynicism, bitching, irony, parody and so on." Bell and de Gama (2018, p. 943) pick up on these ideas to call for practices of "taking a stand in uncritical academic organizations." As they suggest,

> To take a stand is to make a determined effort to resist or fight for something. It implies embodied, enacted presence in a specific place or space – holding one's ground against opposing forces. In taking a stand, the body acts as a physical obstruction which disrupts established norms and provides a means of resistance.
>
> (Bell and de Gama, 2018, p. 940)

We suggest that "taking a stand" in this embodied, enacted way can provide a form of resistance that builds upon the questioning of one's normative orientations and actively orientating differently. It thereby allows us to be affected differently, to be (in) touch(ed) not only with those who fit existing organizational norms.

We believe the journal *Organization*'s recommitment to racial justice in response to the #BlackLivesMatter movement to be a good and illustrative example of "taking a stand" against white superiority, including everyday and institutional racism (Mir and Zanoni, 2020). More concretely, the editors' commitment to taking a stance means that the journal will actively solicit submissions of articles that deal explicitly with anti-Black racism and invite researchers to develop special issues on the matter, in addition to recruiting Black academics to the editorial board and supporting junior Black scholars through the offices of the journal. Adopting Ahmed's concepts, we might claim: To take a stand implies willfully accepting the assignment of becoming affect aliens – as editors, reviewers, authors, supervisors, teachers, and colleagues – as a form of embodied, enacted presence in the organizational settings we inhabit. It implies being willfully orientated differently, or at least stopping ourselves from using our orientation as a straightening device towards "queer moments when objects slip" (Ahmed, 2006c, p. 566). The body becomes a means of resistance by refusing to become a "happy object" for the organization (Ahmed, 2008b). Be it in academia or in other organizational contexts, one might instead turn to "queer use" (Ahmed, 2019) to do otherwise than what is intended, required or demanded; one may become a killjoy, a subject who certainly excels at "cynicism, bitching, irony, parody and so on" (Ashcraft, 2017, p. 44).

Recommended reading

Original text by Sara Ahmed

Ahmed, S. (2014). *The cultural politics of emotion*. 2nd ed. Edinburgh, UK: Durham University Press.

Key academic text

Special issue on Sara Ahmed's work: 'Meeting Again: Reflections on *Strange Encounters* 20 years on' in *Journal of Intercultural Studies*, 2021, ed., V. Marotta, 42(1).

Accessible resource

feministkilljoys – Research blog by Sara Ahmed. Available at https://feministkilljoys.com/

References

Ahmed, S. (1996). Beyond humanism and postmodernism: Theorizing a feminist practice. *Hypatia*, 11(2), pp. 71–93.

Ahmed, S. (2000). *Strange encounters. Embodied others in post-coloniality*. London and New York: Routledge.

Ahmed, S. (2002). This other and other others. *Economy and Society*, 31(4), pp. 558–572.

Ahmed, S. (2004). Affective economies. *Social Text*, 22(2), pp. 117–139.

Ahmed, S. (2006a). Doing diversity work in higher education in Australia. *Educational Philosophy and Theory*, 38(6), pp. 745–768.

Ahmed, S. (2006b). *Queer phenomenology: Orientations, objects, others*. Durham, NC: Duke University Press.

Ahmed, S. (2006c). Orientations: Towards a queer phenomenology. *GLQ: A Journal of Lesbian and Gay Studies*, 12(4), pp. 534–574.

Ahmed, S. (2007). A phenomenology of whiteness. *Feminist Theory*, 8(2), pp. 149–168.

Ahmed, S. (2008a). Open forum imaginary prohibitions. Some preliminary remarks on the founding gestures of the 'new materialism'. *European Journal of Women's Studies*, 15(1), pp. 23–39.

Ahmed, S. (2008b). The politics of good feeling. *Australian Critical Race and Whiteness Studies Association*, 4(1), pp. 1–18.

Ahmed, S. (2009). Happiness and queer politics. *World Picture*, 3.

Ahmed, S. (2010a). Killing joy: Feminism and the history of happiness. *Signs: Journal of Women in Culture and Society*, 35(3), pp. 571–594.

Ahmed, S. (2010b). *The promise of happiness*. Durham, NC, and London, UK: Duke University Press.

Ahmed, S. (2011). Willful parts: Problem characters or the problem of character. *New Literary History*, 42(2), pp. 231–253.

Ahmed, S. (2012). *On being included: Racism and diversity in institutional life*. Durham, NC: Duke University Press.

Ahmed, S. (2014a). Not in the mood. *New Formations*, 82, pp. 13–28.

Ahmed, S. (2014b). *The cultural politics of emotion*. 2nd ed. Edinburgh, UK: Durham University Press.

Ahmed, S. (2014c). *Willful subjects*. Durham, NC: Duke University Press.

Ahmed, S. (2017). *Living a feminist life*. Durham, NC: Duke University Press.

Ahmed, S. (2019). *What's the use? On the uses of use*. Durham, NC: Duke University Press.

Ahmed, S. (2021). Travelling with strangers. *Journal of Intercultural Studies*, 42(1), pp. 8–23.

Ashcraft, K.L. (2017). "Submission" to the rule of excellence: Ordinary affect and precarious resistance in the labour of organization and management studies. *Organization*, 24(1), pp. 36–58.

Basner, K., Christensen, J.F., French, J.E. and Schreven, S. (2018). Snaptivism: A collective biography of feminist snap as affective activism. *Ephemera – Theory & Politics in Organization*, 18(4), pp. 901–922.

Bell, E. and de Gama, N. (2018). Taking a stand: The embodied, enacted and emplaced work of relational critique. *Organization*, 26(6), pp. 935–947.

Borch, C. (2020). Fra individ til masseadfærd: Sådan kan 'sociale laviner' opstå i storbyen [From individual to crowd behaviour: How social avalanches can occur in the metropolis]. *Videnskab.dk*, Feb. 11. Available at: https://videnskab.dk/forskerzonen/kultur-samfund/fra-individ-til-masseadfaerd-saadan-kan-sociale-lavineropstaa-i-storbyen [Accessed 11 Dec. 2020].

Brinkmann, S. (2020). Lykkens idéhistorie [The idea history of happiness]. In: A.B. Sköld and S. Brinkmann, red., *Kampen om Lykken – perspektiver, potentialer og problemer [The fight for happiness – perspectives, potentials and problems]*. Aarhus, DK: Forlaget Klim, pp. 37–62.

Christensen, J.F. (2021). Orange feelings and reparative readings, or how I learned to know alternative organization at Roskilde Festival. *Culture and Organization*, 27(2), pp. 152–170.

Christensen, J.F., Muhr, S.L. and Just, S.N. (2020). Hyphenated voices: The organization of racialized subjects in contemporary Danish public debate. *Organization*. https://doi.org/10.1177/1350508420966739.

Dar, S. and Ibrahim, Y. (2019). The blackened body and White governmentality: Managing the UK academy and the production of shame. *Gender, Work and Organization*, 26, pp. 1241–1254.

Dar, S., Liu, H., Martinez Dy, A. and Brewis, D.N. (2020). The business school is racist: Act up! *Organization*, pp. 1–2. https://doi.org/10.1177/1350508420928521.

Fanon, F. (2008). *Black skin, white masks*. London, UK: Pluto Press.

Gorton, K. (2007). Theorizing emotion and affect – Feminist engagements. *Feminist Theory*, 8(3), pp. 333–348.

Heidegger, M. (1970/1927). *Being and time*. San Francisco: Harper.

Hochschild, A.R. (1983). *The managed heart: Commercialization of human feeling*. Berkeley, CA: University of California Press.

hooks, b. (2000). *Feminist theory: From margin to Centre*. London, UK: Pluto Press.

Husserl, E. (1970/1922). *Logical investigations*. Leiden: Brill Academic Publishers.

Lorde, A. (1984). *Sister outsider: Essays and speeches*. Trumansburg, NY: The Crossing Press.

Mir, R. and Zanoni, P. (2020). Black lives matter: *Organization* recommits to racial injustice. *Organization*. https://doi.org/10.1177/1350508420966740.

Mohanty, C. (1988). Under western eyes: Feminist scholarship and colonial discourses. *Feminist Review*, 30(1), pp. 61–88.

Schmitz, S. and Ahmed, S. (2014). Affect/emotion: Orientation matters. A conversation between Sigrid Schmitz and Sara Ahmed. *Freiburger Zeitschrift für Geschlechter-Studien*, 20(2), pp. 97–108.

Spinoza, B. (2006). *The essential Spinoza: Ethics and related writings*, ed. M. Morgan. Indianapolis and Cambridge: Hackett Publishing Company, Inc.

Spivak, G. (1996/1985). Subaltern studies: Deconstructing historiography. In: D. Landy and G. Maclean, eds., *The Spivak reader*. New York and London: Routledge, pp. 203–236.

Tyler, M. (2019). Reassembling difference? Rethinking inclusion through/as embodied ethics. *Human Relations*, 72(1), pp. 48–68.

Vitry, C. (2020). Queering space and organizing with Sara Ahmed's Queer Phenomenology. *Gender, Work and Organization*. https://doi.org/10.1111/gwao.12560.

Willmott, H. (2013). Reflections on the darker side of conventional power analytics. *Academy of Management Perspectives*, 27(4), pp. 281–286.

3 In the Worlding of Kathleen Stewart

Daydreaming a Conversation With 'SHE'

Silvia Gherardi

Introduction

From the Latin *introducere*, composed of *intro* – to the inside – and *ducere* to lead, the term introduction means to bring a person into a place or group. This is the aim of this short introduction: to introduce you – readers – into a conversation taking place, in an imaginary time and space, between a speaking subject (called *ME*), who is also the writer and the author of this chapter, and another subject (called SHE) who is the textual representation of a writer who signs her writings with the name Kathleen Stewart and who is going to explain herself with the use of the pronoun SHE.

Readers need to be patient because introducing a new person to a group is a delicate matter. They should understand that the group is talking about affect and organization studies, and debating what the latter can bring to the former. Maybe it is useful to know beforehand that the pair's conversation is focused on a specific formulation of affect as 'ordinary affect', meaning that ordinary affects are the varied, surging capacities to affect and to be affected, and this means giving to everyday life the quality of a continual motion of relations, scenes, contingencies and emergences. Therefore, 'ordinary affect' may become a powerful lens for becoming able to look for the everyday in organizational life, its ephemeral qualities, its aesthetics, its sensory textures of connections and subtle movements of change. To become able to see and sense a compositional node. This capacity takes the form of a sharply impassive attunement to the ways in which an assemblage of organizing elements comes to hang together as a 'thing' that has qualities, sensory aesthetics and lines of force: a worlding. Worlding is a way of approaching wholes, systems, networks or culture in ways that account for emergence, the assemblage of disparate entities, and the experience or situation of being 'in' something.

DOI: 10.4324/9781003182887-3

In case I have been able to introduce the readers to the context of the conversation in which they are going to be conducted, now they need some warnings. First, they are introduced to a daydreaming, thus accepting the rules of the blurred line between dream and reality. Secondly, the daydreaming of a conversation between two masquerade authors (SHE and *ME*) that they are going to read is a performative text: it looks like it has 'affect' as an object of conversation, in reality it has the hidden aim of troubling the readers by performing affect.

Daydreaming a conversation

ME: Since I agreed to contribute to this book with a chapter focused on Kathleen Stewart, I suffer (or better I enjoy) daydreaming. Apparently, it is not a worrying symptom. I looked for its definition and found that a daydream is when your mind wanders and your attention shifts from the task at hand to a place that is entirely your own and that daydreams consist of little videos. I confess that, in reading Kathleen Stewart's writings, I always find myself daydreaming about a conversation with her, often an intimate conversation in which we exchange memories. So often in reading her 'small cases', especially those forming the book, *Ordinary Affect*, they resonate with some of my souvenirs from my fieldwork in organizations. In my daydreaming I feel at a visceral level the transmission of affect from the material paper that I am reading and have in my hands, to imagination, to the words that flow inside my closed lips and I tell her how important her work has been in my understanding and theorizing affective ethnography (Gherardi, 2019), as a style of being in the field and becoming-with others. I have so many conversations with her and I tell her a lot of stories that are prompted by her 'scenes' resonating within my experience and my emotions . . . and daydreaming just happens.

SHE[1]: I write not as a trusted guide carefully laying out the links between theoretical categories and the real world, but as a point of impact, curiosity, and encounter. I call myself "she" to mark the difference between this writerly identity and the kind of subject that arises as a daydream of simple presence. "She" is not so much a subject position or an agent in hot pursuit of something definitive as a point of contact; instead, she gazes, imagines, senses, takes on, performs, and asserts not a flat and finished truth but some possibilities (and threats) that have come into view in the effort to become attuned to what a particular scene might offer.

ME: Was this how affect came into your life?

SHE[2]: For me, affect came into view through a slowed ethnographic practice attuned to the forms and forces unfolding in scenes and encounters. This practice pulled the apparatus of conceptualization itself into a tricky alignment with slow ethnography's immanent concerns and with the concerns of the worlds it was trying to trace. Anthropological objects became things that shimmered out of molten states or lay nascent in an atmosphere. They had to be walked around, approached from precise angles, and seen as states of being; they were emergent, or suspended in potentiality, or collapsing, or residual, roosting on live matter as if it were their resting point. The cultural became a resonant and magnetizing field that registered in people and things living through events and conditions. Ethnographic writing began, again, to try to describe collective states and sensibilities hitting people and traversing otherwise incommensurate things: bodies of thought, assemblages of infrastructures and institutions, new ecologies, the rhythms of a daily living, and the strangely connective tissue produced by handheld devices and social media. In the world affect brought into view, the point of analysis was not to track the predetermined *effects* of abstractable logics and structures but, rather, to compose a register of the lived *affects* of the things that took place in a social-aesthetic-material-political worlding.

ME: Here, you are talking of a worlding form of knowing! Your mention of a slow ethnographic practice has an echo in my effort to resist the closure of 'data' and keep open the question of what is cut out from, what does not fit in 'data', what happens in 'not-yet data' beyond the closure in 'data', how data can be otherwise. The conversations with my friend Angelo, and his voice come vividly to me when I think about when we were writing together and how we were doing it together and wondering 'around' how data became data (Benozzo and Gherardi, 2020; Gherardi and Benozzo, 2021). In daydreaming I relive the aesthetic experience of the intonation of his voice, his gaze and his presence in our collaboration through the e-mails that went back and forth and carried our thoughts materialized into words. During that process we were reading and engaging with Lugli's (2006) concept of Wunderkammern and with Maggie MacLure's (2013, p. 228) emphasis on wonder "as an untapped potential in qualitative research". This pastime of gathering very different objects and materials together started in the sixteenth century, and marked the beginning of the phenomenon of Wunderkammern or cabinets of curiosities which brought together various pieces from the world around us, a world deemed wonderful and full of amazing surprises. These are places where things were accumulated and piled up without any clear order and where connections came into being without there having to be a logical reason for them. These connections obey their own laws, and belong to the realm of dreams and wonderment. And only recently I stumbled upon a sentence of yours that recalls the cabinets of curiosities, one that I had not noticed the first time I read *Cultural Poesis*. Isn't it amazing how the aesthetic experience of a collaboration disappears from the written text (Strati, 1992)? And how surprising it is the way certain images of thought chase each other like in a refrain (Stewart, 2010)? Or are they present in the written text, but not visible? Are they just a trace below the surface of the text?

SHE[3]: *Ordinary Affects* tries to slow the quick jump to representational thinking and evaluative critique long enough to find ways of approaching the complex and uncertain objects that fascinate because they literally hit us or exert a pull on us. My story,[4] then, is not an exercise in representation or a critique of representation; rather it is a cabinet of curiosities designed to incite curiosity. Far from trying to present a final, or good enough, story of something we might call "U.S. culture," it tries to deflect attention away from the obsessive desire to characterize things once and for all long enough to register the myriad strands of shifting influence that remain uncaptured by representational thinking.

ME: Yes, you have been able to perform 'stories' that are not 'a good enough story of what's going on' and I have the feeling of having spent all my career in learning how to write articles and chapters which could tell a 'good story'. I wonder what I left out, what I silenced, what I excluded from mattering in my construction of a good story. Are you insinuating that in order to craft an extra-ordinary story I downplay the ordinary? But I have always been fascinated by the ordinary!

SHE[5]: Yes, I do, the ordinary can turn on you!
The ordinary can turn on you.
Lodged in habits, conceits, and the loving and deadly contacts
of everyday sociality, it can catch you up in something bad. Or
good.
Or it can start out as one thing and then flip into something
else altogether.
One thing leads to another. An expectation is dashed or fulfilled.
An ordinary floating state of things goes sour or takes off
into something amazing and good. Either way, things turn out to
be not what you thought they were.

ME: In listening to things that turn out to be not what I thought they were, I have vivid images that now, in my memory, make me laugh but when it took place it made my cheeks blush. What opens in my mind is the image of the eyes of one of my interlocutors when both, at the same time, we realized we had signed a contract for a consultancy project for the development of competences but with the term competence we meant diametrically opposed things implying divergent purposes. We were staring at each other as if we were from planets light years apart. It was a fleeting moment that lasted forever.

SHE[6]:   The ordinary registers intensities – regularly, intermittently, urgently, or as a slight shudder. The ordinary[7] is a circuit that's always tuned in to some little something somewhere. Ordinary scenes[8] can tempt the passer by with the promise of a story let out of the bag.

ME: Very often you write *some*thing and, by italicizing the word some, you cut the word in two parts and you raise a wall of mystery around what this something can be and how it is connected to ordinary affect. I am fascinated by the atmosphere that this *some*thing creates.

SHE[9]:   Ordinary affects are the varied, surging capacities to affect and to be affected that give everyday life the quality of a continual motion of relations, scenes, contingencies, and emergences. They're things that happen. They happen in impulses, sensations, expectations, daydreams, encounters, and habits of relating, in strategies and their failures, in forms of persuasion, contagion, and compulsion, in modes of attention, attachment, and agency, and in publics and social worlds of all kinds that catch people up in something that feels like *some*thing.

ME: When you say 'something that feels like *some*thing' I understand that you point to the moment of emergence, what you name 'poesis' (Stewart, 2005) or creativity. I was writing, and I continue to be fascinated, by the 'something that exceeds the speaking subject' (Gherardi and Strati, 2017). Maybe it is a different something? In the chapter I just mentioned, we assumed (following Deleuze, 1988), that there is always something in excess to being, a "something" in excess to language and to the speaking subject. We were problematizing how language constructs competence as a research object, and were asking what happens when we no longer believe in the language/reality binary relation. We were posing the question of how a more-than-representational approach changes our way of talking about competence. We had experimented with a written/visual text, where a traditional written text, based on the illustration of competence in two episodes, was interrupted by a visual language based on three photographic interludes. The aim of the three interludes was to interrupt the smooth discourse on competence in different practices and to invite empathy in reading. The challenge was to interrupt the rhythm of reading with an invitation to feel the poetry of a visual language. In so doing, we intended to produce the effect of troubling the static, rational, and written representation of competence. Your writings follow a similar attention, both to the emergence of *some*thing in time, and in meaning, and in affect, but also beyond language?

SHE[10]: This is an ethnographic attention, but it is one that is loosened from any certain prefabricated knowledge of its object. Instead, it tracks a moving object in an effort (a) to somehow record the state of emergence that animates things cultural and (b) to track some of the effects of this state of things – the proliferation of everyday practices that arise in the effort to know what is happening or to be part of it, for instance, or the haunting or exciting presence of traces, remainders, and excesses uncaptured by claimed meanings. It talks[11] to the reader not as a trusted guide carefully laying out the perfect links between theoretical categories and the real world but rather as a subject caught in the powerful tension between what can be known and told and what remains obscure or unspeakable but is nonetheless real. Its thoughts are speculative, and its questions are the most basic. What is going on? What floating influences now travel through public routes of circulation and come to roost in the seemingly private domains of hearts, homes, and dreams? What forces are becoming sensate as forms, styles, desires, and practices? What does it mean to say that particular events and strands of affect generate impacts? How are impacts registered in lines of intensity? How are people quite literally charged up by the sheer surge of things in the making? What does cultural poesis look like?

ME: I have the feeling that if I want to catch and to describe what ordinary affect 'does', I need to train myself into a sort of atmospheric attunement to a world that is not, or is not only, my world.

SHE[12]: Attending to atmospheric attunements and trying to figure their significance incites forms of writing and critique that detour into descriptive eddies and attach to trajectories. This is writing and theorizing that tries to stick with something becoming atmospheric, to itself resonate or tweak the force of material-sensory somethings forming up. The effort requires a clearing – a space in which to clear the opposition between representation and reality, or the mind-numbing summary evaluations of objects as essentially good or bad, or the effort to pin something to a social construction as if this were an end in itself. Attending to atmospheric attunements means, instead, chronicling how incommensurate elements hang together in a scene that bodies labor to be in or to get through. In the expressivity of something coming into existence, bodies labor to literally fall into step with the pacing, the habits, the lines of attachment, the responsibilities shouldered, the sentience, of a worlding.

ME: I am wondering how I can create this space intentionally, this space which is an inner clearing in which I suspend judgment, slow down the way I look and feel and actively try to enter another worlding. I am unable to explain it, I know it happens and I know when I have the feeling that it has happened. But to write it in words I have to go back to a form of representation or re-presentation, or . . . ???

SHE[13]: This is a writing and thinking experiment aligned with forms of nonrepresentational theory (Thrift, 2007) including 'weak theory' (Sedgwick, 1997), 'fictocriticism' (Muecke, 2008), and the material semiotics of actor-network theory (Latour, 2007). In the spirit of experiment, these approaches attempt to create new spaces for thinking about and imagining what might be going on. They do this first by trying to dedramatize theory, to loosen the formal narrative binds of a hyperactive story shored by banks of moralism and the heavy presumptions of a proper and automatic relationship between thinking subject, concept, and world. Instead, they might propose a pause, or to try to write theory through stories, or try, through descriptive detours, to pull academic attunements into tricky alignment with the amazing, sometimes eventful, sometimes buoyant, sometimes endured, sometimes so sad, always commonplace labor of becoming sentient to a world's work, bodies, rhythms, and ways of being in noise and light and space (Nancy, 1997). Often they create digressions around quick reductionist claims and explanations into the *cul de sac* of situations in which elements of all kinds assemble into something that feels like something (Berlant, 2010). These things require a kind of haptic description in which the analyst discovers her object of analysis by writing out its inhabited elements in a space and time.

ME: What you say resonates with my experience of writing during the forty days of the first lockdown for COVID-19 when, together with a group of women we engaged in a collective writing experiment (Cozza et al., 2021) about the pandemic as a breakdown in the texture of social practices. Writing then was a practice of solidarity for coping with the trauma, for creating a thinking community and for resisting the social distancing created by the physical distance imposed by the pandemic. I resonate with the words of Laureen Berlant (2010, p. 5) that you quote: "one moves around with a sense that the world is at once intensely present and enigmatic, such that the activity of living demands both a wandering absorptive awareness and hypervigilance that collects the material that might help to . . . maintain one's sea legs" (Stewart, 2011, p. 447). Being a sailor, my body knows very well the physical meaning of sea legs and how this feeling is ordinary once on a boat and can be distressing in other places when it is 'out of place'. During the lockdown my sense of the ordinary was upset and in tension in between absorptive awareness and hypervigilance. I wonder if the heart of an ordinary affect lies in this tension?

SHE[14]: Ordinary affects, then, are an animate circuit that conducts force and maps connections, routes, and disjunctures. They are a kind of contact zone where the overdeterminations of circulations, events, conditions, technologies, and flows of power literally take place. To attend to ordinary affects is to trace how the potency of forces lies in their immanence to things that are both flighty and hardwired, shifty and unsteady but palpable too. At once abstract and concrete, ordinary affects are more directly compelling than ideologies, as well as more fractious, multiplicitous, and unpredictable than symbolic meanings. They are not the kind of analytic object that can be laid out on a single, static plane of analysis, and they don't lend themselves to a perfect, three-tiered parallelism between analytic subject, concept, and world. They are, instead, a problem or question emergent in disparate scenes and incommensurate forms and registers; a tangle of potential connections. Literally moving things – things that are in motion and that are defined by their capacity to affect and to be affected – they have to be mapped through different, coexisting forms of composition, habituation, and event. They can be "seen," obtusely, in circuits and failed relays, in jumpy moves and the layered textures of a scene. They surge or become submerged. They point to the jump of something coming together for a minute and to the spreading lines of resonance and connection that become possible and might snap into sense in some sharp or vague way.

ME: Once again, your words create a line of resonance in my mind and I can vividly see the faces of the students who were attending the last PhD course I gave, when one of them asked me: how can I analyse an emerging object, which appears and disappears in the blink of an eye? A doctoral commission will ask me where is my object of study? I had a hard time in introducing your idea of the generativity of emergent things and went away with the feeling that they would prefer the quiet and reassuring certainty of statistical analysis. What could I have said to convince them?

SHE[15]: A long line of thought from Nietzsche to Foucault, to Spinoza to Deleuze, and contemporary theorists such as Haraway, Taussig, Thrift, Stengers, DeLanda, and Berlant has turned and returned attention to forms emergent in the conduct of life. In this line of thought, the forms and forces immanent to ordinary ways of living are taken as intimate registers of knowledge and power.

ME: Is this what you call a compositional node? As an example of a compositional node you mention New England Red (Stewart, 2015), or the road (Stewart, 2014a), or the beach as a thing (Stewart, 2014b), but why is compositional theory (Stewart, 2013) 'provocative'?

SHE[16]: Compositional theory takes the form of a sharply impassive attunement to the ways in which an assemblage of elements comes to hang together as a thing that has qualities, sensory aesthetics and lines of force and how such things come into sense already composed and generative and pulling matter and mind into a making: a worlding. My provocation[17] is to draw theory, through writing, into the compositional attunement through which people and things venture out into reals. Reals are not the kind of thing that an order of representation simply organizes as truth and dominates but "transversal arrays of qualities or activities which, like musical refrains, give order to materials and situations, human bodies and brains included, as actions undertaken act-back to shape muscles and hone senses" (Anderson and Harrison, 2010, p. 8). This is not the work of imagination on dead matter but a "mattering (that) is about the (contingent and temporary) becoming-determinate (and becoming-indeterminate) of matter and meaning" (Barad, 2010, p. 254). Compositional writing[18] as a non-representational method, then, has to stay nimble in the effort to keep up with the distributed agencies of what's throwing together and falling apart. It is in this practice of trying to follow where things (might) go that habits of attunement become an associational logic.

ME: I understand that a composition is more than just an assemblage. If I take as an example of composition how the flowers and vase are arranged in Van Gogh's painting Sunflowers, my attention is turned to the aesthetic quality of those assembled elements, not to their being thrown together.

When you present the beach as a thing, and as a compelling thing, you point to "Singularities of water, sand, sun, cold, shells, breasts, mold, blue herons, lifeguards, turtles, sharks, swimmers in suits, or a fleet of Portuguese men of war blown into contact with human skin throw worlds into form" (Stewart, 2014b, p. 122). Your wording makes me consider how thinking often arises out of surprising encounters, not an object of recognition but of a fundamental encounter, a worlding that is the effect of differences making a difference.

SHE[19]: Models of thinking that slide over the live surface of difference at work in the ordinary to bottom-line arguments about "bigger" structures and underlying causes obscure the ways in which a reeling present is composed out of heterogeneous and noncoherent singularities. They miss how someone's ordinary can endure or can sag defeated; how it can shift in the face of events like a shift in the kid's school schedule or the police at the door. Such a world[20] is not already laid out on the table, with the only task left being an evaluative one. The turn to affect worried the mantras of structure, mediation, representation, and code that had come to operate as a good-enough shorthand for culture and power. In place of the sheer critique of representation, affect added an affirmative critique that registers surprise at what and how things happen. It waits to see as things unfold in a moment, notes points of contact, recognizes the weight or smell of an atmosphere, or traces the spread of intensities across subjects, objects, institutions, laws, materialities, and species.

ME: A phrase by Donna Haraway that I really like comes to my mind: "Reality is an active verb, and the nouns all seem to be gerunds with more appendages than an octopus" (Haraway, 2003, p. 6). The figure of the octopus and the tentacularity of worlding is for Haraway an active mode of thought. Both of you make explicit use of the noun-as-gerund, thus active worlding is informed by our active engagement with the materiality and context in which events and interactions occur. The simple addition of the suffix 'ing' shifts the world from a being to a doing and using the italics in 'wor*l*ding' stresses how wording is worlding. When we, as researchers, are in the field and my fieldwork takes place within organizing, my ethnographic wording is above all an embodied and enacted process – a way of being in the world – an act of attending to the world. You give the example of the beach as a thing, as an assemblage of affects, effects, conditions, sensibilities and practices, I envisage my encounter with an organizational situation like a beach whose wor*l*ding comes about through the situatedness of the social practices shaping the form of organizing.

SHE[21]: In his essay *The Thing* Martin Heidegger (1971) asks what it might mean to meet the world not as representation, interpretation or raw material for exploitation but as a nearing, a gathering of the ringing between subjects and objects into something that feels like something. To thing is to world. An object that has become a thing is not flat and inert before a voraciously dominant subject but an enigma, a provocation. It is matter already configured (Grosz, 2001).

ME: In my intellectual trajectory, feminist new materialism has been very formative and in particular Barad's concept of matter/mattering gave me the words for talking and writing about the materiality in organizational life not as inert and non-living stuff but as an encounter between the vitality and the obduracy of matter/mattering and human beings. When I write about the everyday mess of organizing, I produce a "thing", a text whose destiny is to leave me and travel alone in the world before meeting a reader to come alive again through this new encounter. In writing I hope to be able to touch the world of this reader and to resonate in her/his world what I have experienced and have shaped in words. Several times (Gherardi, 2017a, 2017b) I have directly asked my potential readers to indulge in reading, to be passive and open to my voice. I had in mind Kurt Wolff's invitation to "surrender and catch" (Gherardi, 2015). To surrender to the world implies that the researcher is not a dispassionate scientist but rather an engaged being that does not remain a detached, outside observer. In fact, the 'surrender' perspective captures an epistemological position in opposition to the official Western consciousness, in which the relationship to the world is not surrender but mastery, control, efficiency, handling, manipulation. Surrender is unforeseeable, unpredictable, it happens, it befalls whereas catch is the object (a concept, a decision, a poem), and the practice of "surrendering-to" involves a conscious effort to promote a relation with a specific phenomenon. I have in mind a rather "passive" positioning, a surrendering to reading, while I have the feeling that instead, you ask for an "active" reading.

SHE[22]: I ask the reader to read actively – to follow along, read into, imagine, digress, establish independent trajectories and connections, disagree. My own voice is particular and partial, tending in this case to be a surreal, dream-like description of ordinary spaces and events. The subject I "am" in the stories I tell is a point of impact meandering through scenes in search of linkages, surges, and signs of intensity. I suppose that the writing gropes toward embodied affective experience.

ME: Therefore, the reader can be both active and passive. I dare to say "actively passive". This reminds me of the exploration of the author's voice in the work by Lisa Mazzei and Alecia Jackson (2017). They move toward positioning voice in qualitative research as a thing that is entangled with other things in an assemblage. They reconfigure voice by refusing the primacy of voice as simply spoken words emanating from a conscious subject and instead place voice within the material and discursive knots and intensities of the assemblage. In this way it becomes possible to de-centre the humanist voice attached to an individual and to account for voice as a material-discursive practice that is inseparable from all human and non-human elements in an assemblage. The researcher is thus inside the research practice as one, among other elements of the assemblage, or how I prefer to write, the *agencement* of elements (Gherardi, 2016). Deleuze and Guattari's (1987) concept of *agencement*, translated in English as assemblage, has been very influential both in your and in my work, not to mention the influence it has had had on post-qualitative research (Coleman and Ringrose, 2013).

SHE[23]: Deleuze and Guattari (1987) polemicized the conflict between meaning-based models of culture and models that track actual events, conjunctures, and articulations of forces to see what they do. In the wake of their critique, they outlined a theory of the affective as a state of potential, intensity, and vitality (see also Guattari, 1995). Contemporary feminist theorists, notably Haraway, Strathern, and Sedgwick, have carefully – and with enormous creative energy of their own – worked to theorize the generativity in things cultural and to make room for ways of thinking and writing it, as has Taussig.

ME: I think that one of the reasons for paying attention to ordinary affects and for not defining affect as an it, is to avoid 'meaning' and instead to look for the intensities they build as they move though bodies and potentialities.

SHE[24]: Yes, the potential . . ..
The potential stored in ordinary things is a network of transfers and relays.
Fleeting and amorphous, it lives as a residue or resonance in an emergent assemblage of disparate forms and realms of life.
Yet it can be as palpable as a physical trace.
Potentiality is a thing immanent to fragments of sensory experience and dreams of presence. A layer, or layering to the ordinary, it engenders attachments or systems of investment in the unfolding of things.

ME: Is the potential lurking behind the reals?

Coda

In music, the Italian word *coda* (tail) names a passage that brings a piece or a movement to an end. The reason for a coda is that, after the climax of the main body of a piece, a coda is required to look back on the main body and allow listeners to reflect. This conversation with Kathleen Stewart is a *collage* that imitates an interactive exchange of thoughts that incorporates not only stylistic elements of her anthropological work but also her own words abstracted from the original writing context (a violence operated on the integrity of a text). As a style of writing, my *collage* is a mechanism of intertextuality in which I stage the intra-actions of a text coming in contact with another text, imitating the interactions between masquerade authors and enlarging the participation in the conversation to other absent-present authors. It is a tool for evoking the debate that characterizes the contemporary era in which we live and in which we world the world.

Acknowledgements: I thank my colleagues Antonio Strati and Marie Manidis, who had the patience to read and comment on a first draft of this chapter. It is understood that the responsibility for the final paper is mine alone.

Notes

1 Stewart, K. (2007). *Ordinary affects*. Durham, NC: Duke University Press, p. 5.
2 Stewart, K. (2017). In the world that affect proposed. *Cultural Anthropology*, 32(2), p. 192
3 Stewart, K. (2007). *Ordinary affects*. Durham, NC: Duke University Press, pp. 4–5.
4 Stewart, K. (2005). Cultural poesis: The generativity of emergent things. In: N.K. Denzin and Y.S. Lincoln, eds., *Handbook of qualitative research*. Los Angeles, CA: Sage, p. 1029.
5 Stewart, K. (2007). *Ordinary affects*. Durham, NC: Duke University Press, p. 106.
6 Stewart, K. (2007). *Ordinary affects*. Durham, NC: Duke University Press, p. 10.
7 Stewart, K. (2007). *Ordinary affects*. Durham, NC: Duke University Press, p. 12.
8 Stewart, K. (2007). *Ordinary affects*. Durham, NC: Duke University Press, p. 23.
9 Stewart, K. (2007). *Ordinary affects*. Durham, NC: Duke University Press, p. 2.
10 Stewart, K. (2005). Cultural poesis: The generativity of emergent things. In: N.K. Denzin and Y.S. Lincoln, eds., *Handbook of qualitative research*. Los Angeles, CA: Sage, p. 1015.
11 Stewart, K. (2005). Cultural poesis: The generativity of emergent things. In: N.K. Denzin and Y.S. Lincoln, eds., *Handbook of qualitative research*. Los Angeles, CA: Sage, p. 1016.
12 Stewart, K. (2011). Atmospheric attunements. *Environment and Planning D: Society and Space*, 29(3), p. 452.
13 Stewart, K. (2011). Atmospheric attunements. *Environment and Planning D: Society and Space*, 29(3), p. 445.
14 Stewart, K. (2007). *Ordinary affects*. Durham, NC: Duke University Press, pp. 3–4.
15 Stewart, K. (2014). Road registers. *Cultural Geographies*, 21(4), p. 549.
16 Stewart, K. (2014). Tactile compositions. In: P. Harvey, E. Casella, G. Evans, H. Knox, C. Mc Lean, E. Silva, N. Thoburn, and K. Woodward, eds., *Objects and materials: A Routledge companion*. London: Routledge, p. 119.

17 Stewart, K. (2013). Studying unformed objects: The provocation of a compositional mode. *Cultural Anthropology website*, June 30, 2013. Available at: https://culanth.org/fieldsights/350-studying-unformed-objects-the-provocation-of-a-compositional-mode.
18 Stewart, K. (2015). New England red. In: P. Vannini, ed., *Nonrepresentational methodologies: Re-envisioning research*. London: Routledge, p. 21.
19 Stewart, K. (2007). *Ordinary affects*. Durham, NC: Duke University Press, p. 4.
20 Stewart, K. (2017). In the world that affect proposed. *Cultural Anthropology*, 32(2), p. 193.
21 Stewart, K. (2014). Tactile compositions. In: P. Harvey, E. Casella, G. Evans, H. Knox, C. Mc Lean, E. Silva, N. Thoburn, and K. Woodward, eds., *Objects and materials: A Routledge companion*. London: Routledge, p. 119.
22 Stewart, K. (2005). Cultural poesis: The generativity of emergent things. In: N.K. Denzin and Y.S. Lincoln, eds., *Handbook of qualitative research*. Los Angeles, CA: Sage, p. 1015.
23 Stewart, K. (2005). Cultural poesis: The generativity of emergent things. In: N.K. Denzin and Y.S. Lincoln, eds., *Handbook of qualitative research*. Los Angeles, CA: Sage, p. 1016.
24 Stewart, K. (2007). *Ordinary affects*. Durham, NC: Duke University Press, p. 21.

Recommended reading

Original text by Kathleen Stewart

Stewart, K. (2007). *Ordinary affects*. Durham, NC: Duke University Press.

Key academic text

Stewart, K. (2011). Atmospheric attunements. *Environment and Planning D: Society and Space*, 29(3), pp. 445–453.

Accessible resource

Romero, A. and Locke, T.A. (2017). Words in worlds: An interview with Kathleen Stewart. *Cultural Anthropology Website*, July 20. Available at: https://culanth.org/fieldsights/words-in-worlds-an-interview-with-kathleen-stewart.

References

Anderson, B. and Harrison, P. (2010). The promise of non-representational theories. In: B. Anderson and P. Harrison, eds., *Taking place: Non-representational theories and geography*. Surrey: Ashgate, pp. 15–48.
Barad, K. (2010). Quantum entanglements and hauntological relations of inheritance: Dis/continuities, spacetime enfoldings and justice-to-come. *Derrida Today*, 3(2), pp. 240–268.

Benozzo, A. and Gherardi, S. (2020). Working within the shadow: What do we do with 'not-yet' data? *Qualitative Research in Organizations and Management*, 15(2), pp. 145–159.

Berlant, L. (2010). *Cruel optimism*. Durham: Duke University Press.

Coleman, B. and Ringrose, J., eds. (2013). *Deleuze and research methodologies*. Edinburgh, UK: Edinburgh University Press.

Cozza, M., Gherardi, S., Graziano, V., Johansson, J. Mondon-Navazo, M., Murgia, A. and Trogal, K. (2021). COVID-19 as a breakdown in the texture of social practices. *Gender, Work and Organization*, 28(S1), pp. 190–208.

Deleuze, G. (1988). *Spinoza: Practical philosophy*. San Francisco: City Lights Books.

Deleuze, G. and Guattari, F. (1987). *A thousand plateaus: Capitalism and schizophrenia*. Minneapolis: University of Minnesota Press.

Gherardi, S. (2015). Why Kurt Wolff matters for a practice-based perspective of sensible knowledge in ethnography. *Journal of Organizational Ethnography*, 4(1), pp. 117–131.

Gherardi, S. (2016). To start practice-theorizing anew: The contribution of the concepts of *agencement* and formativeness. *Organization*, 23(5), pp. 680–698.

Gherardi, S. (2017a). One turn . . . . and now another one. Do the turn to practice and the turn to affect have something in common? *Management Learning*, 48(3), pp. 345–358.

Gherardi, S. (2017b). What is the place of affect within practice-based studies? *M@n@gement*, 20(2), pp. 208–220.

Gherardi, S. (2019). Theorizing affective ethnography for organization studies. *Organization*, 26(6), pp. 741–760.

Gherardi, S. and Benozzo, A. (2021). Shadow organising as dwelling in the space of the 'not-yet'. *Studies in Continuing Education* (43), 296–310. doi:10.1080/0158037X.2021.1900097.

Gherardi, S. and Strati, A. (2017). Talking about competence: That 'something' which exceeds the speaking subject. In: J. Sandberg, L. Rouleau, A. Langley, and H. Tsoukas, eds., *Skillful performance: Enacting expertise, competence, and capabilities in organizations*. Oxford: Oxford University Press, pp. 103–124.

Grosz, E. (2001). The thing. In: *Architecture from the outside: Essays on virtual and real space*. Cambridge, MA: MIT Press, pp. 167–84.

Guattari, F. (1995). *Chaosmosis: An Ethico-aesthetic paradigm*. Bloomington: Indiana University Press.

Haraway, D. (2003). *The companion species manifesto: Dogs, people, and significant otherness*. Chicago: Prickly Paradigm Press (University of Chicago).

Heidegger, M. (1971). The thing. In: M. Heidegger, ed., *Poetry, language, thought*. New York: Harper and Row, pp. 163–186.

Latour, B. (2007). *Reassembling the social*. Oxford: Oxford University Press.

Lugli, A. (2006). *Arte e meraviglia. Scritti sparsi 1974-1995 (Arts and wonder: Collected writings 1974-1996)*. Torino: Umberto Allemandi & Company.

MacLure, M. (2013). The wonder of data. *Cultural Studies↔Critical Methodologies*, 13(4), pp. 228–232.

Mazzei, L.A. and Jackson, A.Y. (2017). Voice in the agentic assemblage. *Educational Philosophy and Theory*, 49(11), pp. 1090–1098.

Muecke, S. (2008). *Joe in the Andamans*. Sydney: Local Consumption Publications.

Nancy, J. (1997). *The sense of the world*. Minneapolis: University of Minnesota Press.

Sedgwick, E. (1997). *Novel gazing*. Durham: Duke University Press.

Stewart, K. (2005). Cultural poesis: The generativity of emergent things. In: N.K. Denzin and Y.S. Lincoln, eds., *Handbook of qualitative research*. Los Angeles, CA: Sage, pp. 1015–1030.

Stewart, K. (2007). *Ordinary affects*. Durham, NC: Duke University Press.

Stewart, K. (2010). Afterword: Worlding refrains. In: M. Gregg and G. Seigworth, eds., *The affect theory reader*. Durham, NC: Duke University Press, pp. 339–354.

Stewart, K. (2011). Atmospheric attunements. *Environment and Planning D: Society and Space*, 29(3), pp. 445–453.

Stewart, K. (2013). Studying unformed objects: The provocation of a compositional mode. *Cultural Anthropology website*, June 30. Available at: https://culanth.org/fieldsights/350-studying-unformed-objects-the-provocation-of-a-compositional-mode.

Stewart, K. (2014a). Road registers. *Cultural Geographies*, 21(4), pp. 549–563.

Stewart, K. (2014b). Tactile compositions. In: P. Harvey, E. Casella, G. Evans, H. Knox, C. Mc Lean, E. Silva, N. Thoburn, and K. Woodward, eds., *Objects and materials: A Routledge companion*. London: Routledge, pp. 119–127.

Stewart, K. (2015). New England red. In: P. Vannini, ed., *Nonrepresentational methodologies: Re-envisioning research*. London: Routledge, pp. 19–33.

Stewart, K. (2017). In the world that affect proposed. *Cultural Anthropology*, 32(2), pp. 192–198.

Strathern, M. (1999). *Property, substance, and effect*. London: Athlone Press.

Strati, A. (1992). Aesthetic understanding of organizational life. *Academy of Management Review*, 17(3), pp. 568–581.

Thrift, N. (2007). *Nonrepresentational theory: Space, politics, affect*. New York: Routledge.

4 In the Web of the Spider-Woman

Towards a New Cosmopolitics of Familiarity and Kinship in Organization (Donna Haraway)

Lindsay Hamilton

Introduction

Social theorist Donna Haraway has pioneered path-breaking lines of enquiry in poststructuralist, postmodernist, postcolonialist and ecofeminist thought. Although not an organization scholar, *per se*, her conceptual arguments speak to important and topical organizational themes, not least of which is the case for seeking out the meaningful inclusion of non-humans in the theorization of commercial activity. These themes are important for those interested in the concept of affect within organizations for they help develop a less human-centric way of viewing relationships and co-dependencies. Her work supports new attention to previously overlooked actors and objects of concern within organizations and in the wider environment: algorithms, cloud data stores, cats, fungi, trees, military drones, plutonium, graphene, robots, soil and water, to name but a few (O'Doherty, 2016). Highlighting the contiguous and relational rather than oppositional nature of differently embodied actors in social life, Haraway's work advocates kinship ties between humans and these 'others'. Scholars engaging with her work call for the inclusion of non-humans in business school outputs (Labatut, Munro and Desmond, 2016), research methods (Hamilton and Taylor, 2017) and pedagogical approaches (Tallberg, Huopalainen and Hamilton, 2020).

Haraway's theorization of the connections between humans and other actors supports new thinking on the meaning and social expression of affect, as a connection, a mutual relationship akin to family or 'nature-culture'; a move which 're-members humans as temporary expressions of, and as made-up of, the same stuff of the worlds they study' (Latimer, 2017, p. 246; Donaldson and Kymlicka, 2011). Decentring humans as all-powerful prime movers, her principal argument is that actors of all kinds – be they human or otherwise – exist in entanglement, enmeshed and affectively connected across time and space. It is our responsibility,

DOI: 10.4324/9781003182887-4

she argues, to see these connections as family ties and apply the same principles of care and reciprocity to commercial activity lay out a template for sustainability.

Human perceptions of the world around them, their ideas about what holds true, are always historically specific, Haraway argues, and so can shift as the body and mind moves through different embodied, geographically and historically specific terrains, relationships or 'situations'. Thus, eschewing both the mythology of human exceptionalism as well as related claims to eternal and exclusively human truths and knowledge systems, her vivid and radical writing critiques the potency of human efforts to dominate and exploit natural resources in damaging extraction and consumption practices. She berates the lack of value placed upon human–animal companionship and affective ties, calling for humans to care for actors of all species rather than reproduce, to consume less and to seek out ways to extract value without violence. Haraway's literary style draws focus to the transhumanity of *affect as kinship*. Affect can exceed of humanistic borders, if kinship is embraced. Several organic metaphors emerge throughout her work such as compost, coral reefs, roots and tentacles; vivid descriptions that empower connections, minglings and tethers rather than divisions. Her approach speaks to contemporary discourses in green accounting, corporate social responsibility and business ethics.

This chapter illuminates a small selection of Haraway's thinking to show how she has implicitly and explicitly influenced a more-than-human strand of organizational scholarship over four decades. The chapter does not seek to mine the technical details of Haraway's many books and articles, nor does it track developments, inconsistencies, or paradoxes in her thinking over time. Instead, the aim is to explore Haraway's particular style of thought to better highlight its value for organizational studies. With that aim in mind, the next section sets out some of the basic principles which undergird Haraway's outlook, then turns to the literary tools through which they are depicted. The chapter concludes with possible future 'moves' that each unfold a glimpse of a future 'Harawavian' way of seeing affect as kinship within organization studies.

Constructing nature: managed difference and blasphemous thinking

At the outset of *Primate Visions*, Haraway (1989) provokes readers to think, 'In what specific places, out of which social and intellectual histories, and with what tools is nature constructed as an object of erotic and intellectual desire?' (p. 1). Her aim in challenging the reader, thus, is to inspect the social and political *nature of nature* and, in doing so, 'set new terms for the traffic between what we have come to know historically as nature and culture' (p. 15). This early provocation problematises assumptions and labels that have perpetuated the symbolic chasms between human culture and the earthy wildness of nature, a state she names 'managed difference' (p. 69). Such differences emerge culturally, for example, in the way natural history museums display the evolutionary narrative with 'man' uppermost in the hierarchy of life. For Haraway, whose (1988) concept of 'situated knowledge' posits the transience and impermanence of even seemingly embedded and perpetual value-systems, there is always hope that what is known, held as normative and embedded in culture, can also shift and change as new situations emerge.

'Tentacular' is a word Haraway uses (2016) to highlight the potential for new knowledge. *Tentacular* emerges from the Latin *tentaculum*, meaning 'feeler', and *tentare*, meaning 'to feel' and 'to try'. If the tentacular is concerned with *tentative* acts of trying and feeling rather than instrumental control, such a metaphor commits an act of intellectual 'blasphemy' in that it runs contra to accepted wisdom about humanity's powerful place within the world (something many business schools pay little or no attention to, even in their most critical scholarship). In Haraway's view, the 'organism is an object of knowledge as a system of the production and partition of energy, or as a system of division of labour with executive functions'. Importantly, here, the organism as an *object of knowledge* only comes into being through *being known*; that is, within a context of 'resource managements, the tracking of energies through trophic layers'.

Knowledge objects (nouns) and knowledge acts (verbs) work through classificatory practices which perpetuate a false dichotomy between observer and observed. Haraway argues that an act of blasphemy is needed if we are to unpick the culturally and politically settled state of artificial separation. Blasphemy is a term used here not in the sense of religious dissent, but 'category deviance', a form of radical questioning of the taxonomies and classificatory practices that have sought to keep politics, science and technology separate. Haraway desires a 'traffic' between human knowledge and the world 'out there', which involves taking note of organisms, technologies, spaces and organizations and working out what they do, how they relate, how they are coded and changed. She considers close-up scrutiny to have the potential to helpfully unmanage the 'managed difference' that shores up human–nature hierarchies and actively supports the exploitation of non-humans as resources (Hamilton and Taylor, 2013). It is the precursor to embracing the values and implications of affective connections and entangled agencies thriving across boundaries.

Haraway takes the practice of questioning difference into the domain of technologies too. In *The Cyborg Manifesto* (1991a), she brings together the flesh and machine that increasingly underpins human life and radically opens out the debate on categories warning of the dangers of 'deifying' boundaries, borderlines and typological definitions. Perhaps, she states, we are inhabiting an 'intersectional world' wherein we inhabit multiple categories simultaneously. This does not imply the dissolving of meaningful labels (male and female, for example, see 1995) but rather the radical questioning of their social 'torque' or driving power. Labels hold the power to take us somewhere. In the process of being driven by categories and their names, humans become 'components' within a 'system architecture whose basic modes of operation are probabilistic' (Haraway, 1991a, p. 212): a state of affairs she aims to challenge. In other words, torque is the power that turns the label of 'humanity' into a social force; a potency that carries real-life effects.

Returning to the notion of kinship as a form of affect gives us a way of unroving the driving practices of categorization. In Haraway's (1994) perspective, kinship is a form of intense, inherited, sometimes temporary (or difficult) attachment: a mode of existence with others in the world. Striving for affective connections with others can also function as a motivating goal for unmaking traditional norms, fixed categories and thereby de-sanctifying their power; their social torque. Although aiming to unmake and unbind categories, Haraway (2008, 2004) is not seeking destruction but – in fact – a more accurate recognition of the messy overlapping agencies that co-constitute social life and form connections between people, animals and other forms of agency. As recent events have unfolded during the COVID-19 pandemic, for example, many who have traditionally worked in human-centred office spaces have transitioned to online meetings, thereby witnessing the important role that domestic companion animals play in providing emotional warmth and comfort as well as breaking down communicative barriers between colleagues. Here, animal actors – always present in the 'backstage' region of the *work self* – emerge from the shadows as integral, closely connected and enmeshed in the daily patterns of the home.

Haraway's (1991b) focus upon the political materialities of information, organization and category maintenance asks questions about the material of the world rather than moving beyond it in some sort of utopian 'beyonding' or 'reworlding'. Hence Haraway's view of kinship is not about proposing a state of futuristic posthumanism in which we are indistinguishable from robots, cats or soil and she is reticent about the common use of the prefix, 'post' in her critical theory on humanity. She perceives a danger in that label too (1994, 1995, 2008, 2004). The *Companion Species Manifesto* (2003) interrogates relationalities where the absolute meanings attached to the label of 'species' are in question.

She considers how emotional or affective relations with non-human others – such as those observed by colleagues during a video conference – embrace new 'becomings'.

More accurate than adopting a pretence of strict humanism that excludes different animals from everyday processes, including work, 'becomings' accept and highlight the value of affect through kinship. Kinship, for Haraway is a binding, formed through the unbinding of difference. As Haraway explains (2003, p. 34), if you have a kin member, a family member, 'they have you: you can make claims on each other'. Kinship is about a kind of non-optional reciprocity. Kinship relations are a state of living or dying in solidarity with other beings (human or non-human) where they 'have stakes in each other'. If one has a dog, her argument goes, care must be provided; as failure to offer basic care needs would be deemed a failing as the domestic world as to function in togetherness.

The way Haraway presents human–material, human–technology and human animal relations is blasphemous in the sense that her work unravels the cleanly purified categories that hold up the world (and the business world in particular). Far beyond a simple story of 'man and tool' through history, but rather her work is concerned with challenging and eroding the very categories that constitute 'self' and 'other' – the definitional work that makes primitive labels such as 'man' and 'tool' understandable but which problematises an ethos of connected community. She wants us to pay attention to how all the boundaries in place that hide our connectivity, our interdependency and our relationality are themselves webbed. The boundaries her work challenges are between the literary and the scientific, affect and effect for 'Haraway's writing makes possible a vision in which every move we make, every step we take, everything we create is underpinned by the historicity of how these divisions are enacted' (Latimer, 2017, p. 249).

All the meanings that become attached to different social and cultural categories have roots as well as tentacles, in the sense that they have a source and provenance as well as relational connectivity and reach. This is named an 'affirmatory biopolitics' after Esposito (2008), a condition that downplays otherness and division, and that produces a vision of earthy materiality (which she terms 'compost') rather than confusing free-floating relativism. For Haraway, 'human' is not the same as 'dog' or 'robot' but it is important to think carefully about what the labels 'dog', 'human' and 'robot' enact, how they function to bring together or repel. Other uses different names and terms, each name emerging from different ways of seeing the same concept; 'cosmopolitics' (Stengers, 1997), actor networks (Alcadipani and Hassard, 2010), Gaia (Waddock, 2011), a 'life with new entities' (Latour, 2004a).

Organic metaphors of roots, tentacles and compost present a literary but powerful challenge to the thinking style that supports theories of human progress, strategy and change management. Many critical scholars have drawn on the language of entanglement, affect or actor network theory, for example, to express how heterogeneous sets of 'actants' perform in organizations without normative assumptions of mastery or managerial efficacy (Alcadipani and Hassard, 2010; O'Doherty, 2016; Plumwood, 1993). A good case in point is the science laboratory (Latour and Woolgar, 1992) in which mundane work functions, materials and objects get enlisted in the powerful performance of an ostensibly 'value-free' science that seeks to obscure the creative hand of humans in managing the scholarly publication of results in high-ranking journals. Here workplace assemblies enact objects to give voice and potency to them: a petri dish can be an actor, as can white coats and mould cultures. This lateral view of the organization and its relational experiences is extended by Haraway's powerful writing. For Haraway, voice and potency are not necessarily human.

Welcoming demons, familiars and mysterious entities

For those working in organizational studies, such an approach to relationships and actors could be used to incorporate a 'cosmos' of others in political accounts of work and organizing (Alcadipani and Hassard, 2010; Latour, 2004b), to give rise to inclusive treatment of 'new entities' that they may be 'detected, welcomed and given a shelter' (Latour, 2004b, p. 224) in organizational theory and practice. Such an ethos is emboldened by Haraway's work which frequently draws focus to a mysterious or important non-human actor to perform such acts of 'welcoming'. Across the spectrum of her collected work the characters of cyborg, spiderwoman, vampire, modest witness, FemaleMan, and OncoMouse gather up the ways that movements, techniques and systems of knowledge have rewired many of our apprehensions and experiences of our bodies and 'true selves'. Haraway's metaphoric 'demons' or 'familiars' are often borrowed from folklore, iconography, culture, myth and fable. She remakes her metaphors to suit her purpose.

In setting out her tentacular agenda (2016), for example, Haraway draws our gaze to the invented character of a spider that she names, *Pimoa Cthulhu*, who dwells in the redwood forests of North Central California. 'Cthulhu' emerges from the word chthonic (a classical Greek word meaning, 'of the earth') which echoes Haraway's preference for organic, earthy metaphors but also plays on tropes found in earlier science fiction stories about tentacular monsters interacting with humans. The imagery and location of the spider is analytically valuable for it embodies, quite literally, the idea of the roaming tentacular suggestive of 'tangles, probing creepers, swelling roots, reaching and climbing tendrilled ones'. This imagery stresses that seeking and forming affective networks and types of kin leads to a rich social experience; of 'life lived along lines – and such a wealth of lines – not at points, not in spheres' but instead, 'a series of interlaced trails' made up of wayfarers, characters, beings.

Through the imagery of the leggy, woodland dwelling spider, Haraway quests into the very nature of being human and human being. Affect generated by and within kinship ties – 'not at points, not in spheres' – but extending in 'interlaced trails' is essential to reconfiguring even the most apparently 'immutable' elements of humanity; bodies, bones, blood and genomes. All of these labels can be rethought, repurposed and reworked. The things we often see as signs of our own species distinction and otherness, she proposes, can be reconsidered emblems of a symbiotic system that connects rather than disconnects us from 'nature' (Haraway, 1997). We are also 'feeling', 'probing' and 'trying' just like the woodland spider's leg. Should we embrace a life on the forest floor, perhaps, and eschew the sanitized trappings of the executive lounge (O'Doherty, 2017), the call centre or the open plan office? These are spaces which traditionally demarcate a human from an animal through sanitized lines of sight that offer protection from soil, spiders and interlaced trails that lead us away from the familiar. Haraway wants us to consider ourselves in an entangled web through which other beings are connected.

The visual and literary nature of Haraway's writing develops through the metaphor of compost. Compost is, of course, a material whereby matter has broken down and reformed as a new type of matter. It is an image that applies well to academic work, for instance, a process by which new ideas are always indebted to the painstaking review and critique of the manifold writings and readings that have come before; their breaking down and disintegration allowing for new forms and styles to emerge (Helmreich, 2021). Haraway is not in search of linear progress, here, but rather using compost to underline what she perceives as a more accurate reading of the messy enmeshing or layering of ideas, bodies, labels – new upon old – as an organic and earthy process (Haraway, 2000). In *Staying with the Trouble: Making Kin in the Chthulucene* (2016) she writes, 'Staying with the trouble requires making oddkin; we require each other in unexpected collaborations and combinations, in hot compost piles. We become-with each other or not at all' (p. 4). Although it is not stipulated whether in the metaphor the notion of hot compost piles may be made of leaf matter or coffee grounds, pieces of newspaper, potato peelings or anything else, the purpose is to emphasise the mingling that eventually

produces a rich soil. Rich soil, in turn, can be used to fertilize and reproduce goodness. This idea resonates strongly with critical management
approaches to the 'messy' realities of acts of organising which are seldom
arrived at *ex nihilo*. It also frames her contribution to the theorization of
affect.

The sentiment of mingling and mutuality is what matters here and
returns us to the important anchoring framework of affective kinship
bonds. Indeed, 'oddkin' infers relationships with non-humans, 'others'
who are *not like us*; spiders, leaves and fungi. Haraway frames such relationships and our 'becoming with each other' as 'staying' with the trouble. The nature of 'staying with' is difficult to combine practically with
the physical decline involved in the process of decomposition but the
idea is a call for us to recognise that if we 'become-with each other',
fruitful new kinship links may be formed. In her collection of investigations touching on primates, companion species and technologies, Haraway sets out a (feminine) vision that seeks to question the 'how' and the
'why' of the categories that divide flesh from circuit-boards, animals from
humans, genomes from whole bodies (Latimer, 2017). Throughout the
broad catalogue of work, her aim is to ask by what means such categories get their power and in doing that, to search out new templates of
interaction, mutual mindedness, affective relationships with whatever and
whoever we desire.

Haraway's concerns relate to how organic and fleshy realities are
enacted: she recognises that things could be 'otherwise' and that realities
are not 'destiny' (Law, 2007). The overarching project is to return us to
the fleshy dwellings so long eschewed by Aristotelian and Cartesian pre-
cepts; to reunite humans with other actors along a continuum of being
that embraces proximity and affect and, in so doing, rejects old tenets of
exceptionalism, hierarchy and progress. Dwelling in new kinship bonds,
accepting that affect is important, she presents humans as the fusty leaves
and mouldering lives of the forest floor: as 'humus', by which bodies,
ideas and paradigms mingle and turn to compost.

The dank and musty imagery of humus and warm compost on the forest floor will be, for many organizational thinkers, a strange and witchy
metaphor to work with. Yet, the concept has resonance for those interested in developing ideas about affect at work; it prompts thought about
connections and relations at a local and a global level. In describing her
forest spider – woman's dwelling place, for example, Haraway (2016)
notes, 'Nobody lives everywhere; everybody lives somewhere' (p. 345).
'This spider is in place, has a place, and yet is named for intriguing travels
elsewhere.' Just as many organizational theorists embrace the located –
ness of the organization as the empirical mainstay of their enquiries – the

office, the call centre, the clinic – Haraway's embraces both the forest – floor as well as the broader possibilities of 'travels elsewhere': a useful and beautiful metaphor to work with. These travels, unfolding like the arachnidian limbs of Pimoa Cthulhu, empower a linguistic, theoretical, methodological extension of thinking on intimacies, connections and impacts and – at a broader 'travelling' level – provoke deeper enquiries (and blasphemies) into the dominant, *global* norms of human exceptionalism and organizational mastery.

Harawavian thinking has become more relevant in subject areas such as corporate social responsibility, business ethics and green accounting (among other disciplines) as we live through the visible impact of climate change, extinctions and zoonotic disease pandemics. There is increasing pragmatic as well as philosophical acceptance that humanist bias in business and management scholarship (Heikkurinen et al., 2019; Hoffman and Jennings, 2021), is integral to make genuine and positive differences to the future security of non-human ecosystems.

As Tallberg et al. (2021, p. 2) state, 'If we agree that the ecological challenges affecting organizations are the result of anthropocentric value-creation models based on profit maximisation, then it may not only be short-sighted but also unethical to limit managerial practice and decision-making exclusively to humans'. Working with the concept that humans exist on a continuum or as Haraway puts it, a web – like mesh in which a vibration in one segment will have reverberation throughout, choices such as consumption patterns, our behaviours and decision making could lead to a radical reconfiguration of what we should eat, where we should travel and how we should conduct ourselves more generally in the world. Taking inspiration from such arguments, in the next and concluding section I extend 'spidery legs' out across a couple of *lines of travel*. The aim is to set out ways for organization studies to apply Haraway's ethos in practical endeavours.

Unfolding spider – legs and intriguing travels

Haraway's conceptualization of affect as kinship works contra to the taken-for-granted nature of 'real-world' definitions, labels and taxonomies. For Haraway, many definitions and labels perpetuate the destructive unbinding of potential kinship ties, working against the benefits of affective connection. Indeed, she goes further. Labels can imbue a sort of violence that allows exploitative practices and power imbalances to remain unchallenged. Haraway expresses 'rage' at the ways that myths have perpetuated human–nature division and, thereby, commercial exploitation. Haraway is vocal and explicit about what this means – in her words, 'the scale of burning ambitions of fossil-making man' with all the other 'accelerating extractions of minerals, plant and animal flesh, human homelands, and so on' she terms, quite bluntly, 'madness'.

Hers is not a philosophical agenda, then, but an emotive and deeply personal quest to advocate for new language practices that build alternatives to the historic ways that humans have defined (and prioritized) their economic activity and gain over other actors, subjugated as 'food', 'vermin' and 'resources'. Knowledge of the world, Haraway argues, 'is always an engaged material practice and never a disembodied set of ideas' (Haraway, 2004, pp. 199–200). Words carry power. Hence, her writing demands a focus on the roots and the potency of labels, the embodied source of the meanings they confer and the socio-political actions they support. It is difficult to accept affective ties, let alone the prospect of kinship with an actor labelled as 'vermin', after all.

If what humans know is 'embedded' in a situation, and empowered through language, then organizational scholarship should not leave labels and categories unscrutinized. For example, the concept of 'Personal Assistant' works with, and implies knowledge of, the distinct category of 'executive' and the category of 'leader' instates the separate and subordinate characteristics of 'follower'. These are just a few of the meaning-laden categories which could be questioned, unmade and which are never a fixed 'destiny' (Law, 2007).

Haraway invites us to see how all human techno-scientific invention and creativity are enrolled in acts of power that can include or exclude various actors and, all the while, remakes the myth of human exceptionality. Any claims to categorical purity (be they racial, gendered, human) need to be held up for inspection. There is importance in applying this style of thought to such familiar terms as 'leader', 'executive' and 'manager' but there is a broader urgency as recent events have underlined the need to preserve and cherish the stuff of our planet; what Eduardo Kohn (2013) calls ecologies of selves, meshworks and overlaps between all creatures, materials and forms. Scrutinising the use of language, labelling particularly, is vital to unmake the categories that perpetuate the species distinction and entrap organizational scholarship in a paradigm that sees non-humans as objects.

Millions of humans and animals work side by side and many empirical investigations already show that animals are not beyond human organising but are rather a constituent part of such organising (Hannah and Robertson, 2017; Sage et al., 2016). For organization studies, this necessitates a consideration of the interactions and interests of non-humans (Wünderlich et al., 2021) as well as the possibilities for what Coulter (2016) helpfully terms *interspecies solidarity* – an ethos for exploring the contiguous and messy connections – rather than disconnections – that work to disempower both humans and other creatures. Calarco (2015) calls for an *ethic of cohabitation* whereby assisting animals and learning from them is set against efforts to manage or extract value from them. The ideas of collaboration, cohabitation and coproduction open out new ontological possibilities for understanding other 'critters' (Helmreich, 2021) and our relationships to them through organizational settings.

In *positive organizational scholarship* (or POS), for instance, the emphasis upon understanding human thriving through acts of empathy and noticing suffering could be extended by the development of models for encouraging noticing, empathising and acting for non-humans. The notion of 'thriving' is readily reconfigured by reference to Haraway's contributions as a more-than-human state to which we should orientate. Non-human inclusivity in *stakeholder theory* is another potential line of theorization, currently tethered to a worldview in which non-humans are considered only insofar as they have a direct instrumental value to humans (Heikkurinen et al., 2019; Waddock, 2011) but which is being reconfigured through an ecofeminist lens (Tallberg, García-Rosell and Haanpää, 2021) inspired by Haraway's thinking. Theoretical travel beyond the human is possible for organizational theorists and Haraway provides the template for doing so.

Her work offers an alternative to 'managerial, technocratic, market-and-profit besotted, modernizing, and human-exceptionalist business-as-usual commitments of so much Anthropocene discourse' (2016, p. 320), a form of thinking that she depicts as 'wrong-headed and wrong-hearted'. The aim is to promote a powerful caring for other worlds. It is time, Haraway states, to rid ourselves of the 'enslavement to Progress and its evil twin, Modernization'. If capitalism was relationally made and empowered through acts of labelling, it can be unmade. We must 'reworld, reimagine, relive, and reconnect with each other, in multispecies well-being'. These points provide a cornerstone for critical organization studies to go further in its attempts to 'feel', 'sense' and explore new possibilities. Haraway stresses the importance of limiting human reproductive potential, 'limiting our numbers' and 'scaling back' our activities in the hope of 'a higher, more inclusive freedom and quality of life'. This speaks to – and against – normative business constructs such as growth, progress and innovation.

If all knowledge-making is political and 'embedded', we need enquiries and experiments in organization studies that counter the silencing of certain actors and forms of action (Gane and Haraway, 2006). The aim should therefore be to recognise, describe and understand the *affective links* that make new forms of kinship bonds rather than reproducing the neat taxonomic categories that differentiate and divide actors (Tallberg,

Huopalainen and Hamilton, 2020). While some might say that we should eschew attempts to know the un – knowable and that questions about kinship and affect between humans and non-humans are woolly, indeterminate and hard to measure, even a basic reappraisal of categorical labels could foster the kind of new thinking that Haraway proposes in searching out overlaps, entanglements and connections. Accepting that there are uncertainties and forms of knowledge that are mysterious, in the interests of recognising affect and kinship bonds Haraway is eager for us to challenge the limitation of what and how we learn.

Her unique contribution is, I consider, built upon a way of seeing the world as a 'cosmopolitics' in which actors of various types might be perceived to be a part of a 'contingent system' (O'Doherty, 2016; Stengers, 2010) that does not seek to perpetuate long-standing distinctions on the basis of what has hitherto been treated as an irreducible essence but instead considers organization as an ecology of practices that takes into account the political and 'tentacular' nature of human interactions, the constraints and obligations such practices impose, and the impact they have on commercial and social lives. Specifically, then, Haraway's contribution offers the opportunity to think deeply about the way that arbitrary, cultural acts of partition, definition and division support oppression and calls for a close eye to the social torque by which categories and labels are produced and reproduced.

Haraway shows that in the nexus of entanglements between how division and labelling is done are possibilities for reproduction of asymmetrical power relations, including capitalism's worst excesses of war and oppression as well as the myriad injustices that pepper organization life; prejudice, discrimination, dominance. When we read the breadth of her manifestos, interviews, essays, conversations and articles together, she offers us a *different way of doing organization* and a different way of theorising affect: not as something akin to emotional connection between humans, but as a deeply ingrained value of tentacular 'feeling' across actors who may form kinship bonds irrespective of their denoted 'labels'. This agenda urges us to see organizational and resource hierarchies differently.

The whole point is to feel, reach out and find different ways of thinking, writing and doing as at the same time connecting things up that are usually held apart. Of course, critiques of instrumental capitalism and simple dualisms have always been present in critical business and management scholarship and many theoretical perspectives (e.g. Marxism, ecofeminism, critical theory, poststructuralism, postcolonialism, posthumanism among others) have honed important critiques of, for instance, financial systems and 'greed', climate and sustainability crisis, and continuing 'wicked' injustices in society (Grint, 1991), all of which carry serious ethical implications for the way that business schools in particular (Parker, 2002) have invested in – and promoted – rational and instrumental ideals of leadership and scientific management in their pedagogies and outputs. Such work has questioned the embedded narratives of progress and development that perceive every problem to be 'solvable given the right technology' (Strathern, 1991); a view predicated on historic discourses of mastery, dominance and reason. Enthusiasm for Haraway's thinking does not detract from the strength of these different endeavours, rather her ideas compliment, scaffold and extend attempts to see management and organization in terms of the kinship bonds that may tether its actors together.

Haraway's more recent work has not been without harsh critique. Lewis (2017), for example, sees Haraway's latter work as worrying in its tendency towards 'anti-maternalism' and 'anti-humanism' rather than anti-exceptionalism:

> As she repeatedly drums home, don't make babies – as much as make kin – becomes the take-home injunction for the reader of Donna Haraway. The vision of trans-species Gemeinschaft that emerges is not so much post- as anti-human.

The charge of anti-humanism is of course a philosophical one (Esposito, 2008), but other critics undermine her writing as weird and psychedelic, hard to read, understand or work with. They have also questioned what, precisely, is so valuable about a tentacular approach to humans as nature-cultures. Yet Haraway's entire argument is not to get 'hung up' on words but to embrace feelings, affective resonance and to take materials, technologies and other species into kinship bonds. Whether Haraway's lucid, literary style is a help or a hindrance for those in the business school, at the very least her powerful questioning of traditional distinctions between human and animal, natural and social, modern and archaic, the scientific and the irrational holds emancipatory potential for enveloping actors of various types and species into new forms of organizational scholarship on affect. To realise the potential of these provocative thoughts, perhaps we should imagine ourselves on the forest floor – as humus, as a mouse or as a spider: the point is to question accepted wisdom and think like kin.

Recommended reading

Original text by Donna Haraway

Haraway, D. (2016). *Staying with the trouble: Making Kin in the Chthulucene*. Durham, NC: Duke University Press.

Key academic text

Schneider, J. (2005). *Donna Haraway: Live theory*. London: A&C Black (Bloomsbury Publishing).

Accessible resource

Gane, N. (2006). When we have never been human, what is to be done? Interview with Donna Haraway. *Theory, Culture & Society*, 23(7–8), pp. 135–158.

References

Alcadipani, R. and Hassard, J. (2010). Actor-network theory, organizations and critique: Towards a politics of organizing. *Organization*, 17(4), pp. 419–435.

Calarco, M. (2015). *Thinking through animals. Identity, difference, indistinction*. Stanford: Stanford University Press.

Coulter, K. (2016). *Animals, work, and the promise of interspecies solidarity*. London: Palgrave Macmillan.

Donaldson, S. and Kymlicka, W. (2011). *Zoopolis: A political theory of animal rights*. Oxford: Oxford University Press.

Esposito, R. (2008). *Bı'os: Biopolitics and philosophy*, trans. T Campbell. Minneapolis: University of Minnesota Press.

Gane, N. and Haraway, D. (2006). When we have never been human, what is to be done? Interview with Donna Haraway. *Theory, Culture & Society*, 23(7–8), pp. 135–158.

Grint, K. (1991). *The sociology of work*. Cambridge: Polity.

Hamilton, L. and Taylor, N. (2013). *Animals at work*. Boston and Lieden: Brill Academic Press.

Hamilton, L. and Taylor, N. (2017). *Ethnography after humanism: Power, politics and method in multi-species research*. London: Palgrave-Macmillan.

Hannah, D. and Robertson, K. (2017). Human-animal work: A massive, understudied domain of human activity. *Journal of Management Inquiry*, 26(1), pp. 116–118.

Haraway, D. (1988). Situated knowledges: The science question in feminism and the privilege of partial perspective. *Feminist Studies*, 14(3) (Autumn), pp. 575–599.

Haraway, D. (1989). *Primate visions: Gender, race and nature in the world of modern science*. New York: Routledge.

Haraway, D. (1991a). A cyborg manifesto: Science, technology and socialist feminism in the late twentieth century. In: *Simians, cyborgs, and women: The reinvention of nature*. London: Free Association Books.

Haraway, D. (1991b). *Simians, cyborgs, and women: The reinvention of nature*. London: Free Association Books.

Haraway, D. (1994). Universal donors in a vampire culture, or it's all in the family: Biological kinship categories in the twentieth-century United States. In: W. Cronon, ed., *Uncommon ground: Toward reinventing nature*. New York: Norton, pp. 321–366.

Haraway, D. (1995). 'Foreword' to women writing culture. In: G.A. Olson and E. Hirsch, eds.. Albany: State University of New York Press, pp. x–xii.

Haraway, D. (1997). *Modest_Witness@Second_Millennium. FemaleMan©_Meets_Onco-MouseTM*. London and New York: Routledge.

Haraway, D. (2000). *How like a leaf, an interview with Thyrza Nichols Goodeve*. New York: Routledge.

Haraway, D. (2003). *The companion species manifesto*. Chicago: Prickly Paradigm.

Haraway, D. (2004). *Crystals, fabrics, and fields: Metaphors that shape embryos*. Foreword by Scott F. Gilbert. Reprint Version. Berkeley: North Atlantic Books (first edition, 1976).

Haraway, D. (2008). *When Species Meet*. Posthumanities Volume 3. Minneapolis: University of Minnesota Press.

Haraway, D. (2016). Tentacular thinking: Anthropocene, capitalocene, chthulucene. In: D Haraway, ed., *Staying with the trouble: Making kin in the chthulucene*. Durham: Duke University Press.

Heikkurinen, P., Clegg, S., Pinnington, A.H., Nicolopoulou, K. and Alcaraz, J.M. (2019). Managing the anthropocene: Relational agency and power to respect planetary boundaries. *Organization & Environment*. https://doi.org/10.1177/1086026619881145.

Helmreich, S. (2021). How like a reef: Figuring coral, 1839–2010. Available at: http://reefhelmreich.blogspot.com/ [Accessed 31 Mar. 2021].

Hoffman, A.J. and Jennings, P.D. (2021). Institutional-political scenarios for Anthropocene society. *Business & Society*, 60(1), pp. 57–94.

Kohn, E. (2013). *How forests think: Toward an anthropology beyond the human*. Berkeley: University of California Press.

Labatut, J., Munro, I. and Desmond, J. (2016). Animals and organizations. *Organization*, 23(3), pp. 315–329.

Latimer, J. (2017). Review: Donna J Haraway, Manifestly Haraway: The cyborg manifesto, the companion species manifesto, companions in conversation (with Cary Wolfe). *Theory, Culture & Society*, 34(7–8), pp. 245–252.

Latour, B. (2004a). *Politics of nature: How to bring the sciences into democracy*. Cambridge, MA: Harvard University Press.

Latour, B. (2004b). Whose cosmos, which cosmopolitics? Comments on the peace terms of Ulrich Beck. *Common Knowledge*, 10(3), pp. 450–462.

Latour, B. and Woolgar, S. (1979/1992). *Laboratory life: The social construction of scientific facts*. Beverly Hills: Sage.

Law, J. (2007). *Actor network theory and material semiotics*. Available at: www.heterogeneities.net/publications/LawANTandMaterialSemiotics.pdf [Accessed 5 Sept. 2007].

Lewis, S. (2017). Cthulhu plays no role for me. *Viewpoint Magazine*. Available at: https://viewpointmag.com/2017/05/08/cthulhu-plays-no-role-for-me/ [Accessed 31 Mar. 2021].

O'Doherty, D. (2016). Feline politics in organization: The nine lives of Olly the cat. *Organization*, 23(3).

O'Doherty, D. (2017). *Reconstructing organization: The loungification of society*. London: Palgrave Macmillan.

Parker, M. (2002). *Against management: Organization in the age of managerialism*. Cambridge: Polity.

Plumwood, V. (1993). *Feminism and the mastery of nature*. New York: Routledge.

Sage, D., Justesen, L., Dainty, A., Tryggestad, K. and Mouritsen, J. (2016). Organizing space and time through relational human–animal boundary work: Exclusion, invitation and disturbance. *Organization*, 23(3), pp. 434–450.

Stengers, I. (1997). *Power and invention: Situating science*. Minneapolis, MN: University of Minnesota Press.

Stengers, I. (2010). *Cosmopolitics I*, trans. R. Bononno. Minneapolis: University of Minnesota Press.

Strathern, M. (1991). *Partial connections*. Savage, MD: Rowman and Littlefield Publishers.

Tallberg, L., García-Rosell, J.C. and Haanpää, M. (2021). Human–animal relations in business and society: Advancing the feminist interpretation of stakeholder theory. *Journal of Business Ethics*. Online first at https://doi.org/10.1007/s10551-021-04840-1 [Accessed 24 May 2021].

Tallberg, L., Huopalainen, A. and Hamilton, L. (2020). Can methods do good? Ethnology and multi-species research as a response to COVID-19. *Ethnologia Fennica*, 47(2), pp. 103–112.

Waddock, S. (2011). We are all stakeholders of Gaia: A normative perspective on stakeholder thinking. *Organization & Environment*, 24(2), pp. 192–212.

Wünderlich, N.V., Mosteller, J., Beverland, M.B., Downey, H., Kraus, K., Lin, M.H. and Syrjälä, H. (2021). Animals in our lives: An interactive well-being perspective. *Journal of Macromarketing*, 34, p. 369.

5 Jane Bennett

Marvelling at a World of Vibrant Matter

Justine Grønbæk Pors

Introduction

This chapter begins with breathing. Inhale. Exhale. Breathing as the coming and going of air, molecules, ideas, scents, affects, and tiny little drops of liquid. Influx. Efflux.[1] While breathing is sometimes used in self-technologies such as, for example mindfulness to stabilize a sense of self, thinking about *who one is* while breathing may also inspire wonderings about the dependence of the human body on its environment. Inhale. Exhale. What comes in when you inhale? How are you affected by the environment in which you live and breathe? What is a self? Our bodies are inhabited by millions of bacteria. Human cells make up only 43% of the body's total cell count (Sender, Fuchs and Milo, 2016). The rest is microbes. Bacteria enter our bodies from the outside and make a home in us. When we digest our lunch or when our immune systems fight a threat, these are processes in which bacteria play a leading role. Inhale. Exhale. What do you notice? Even our moods are not just our own or strictly human as bacteria also play a role in regulating them. As Jane Bennett (2020, p. xi) puts it: 'A swarm of non-humans are at work *inside* and *as* us; we are powered by a host of inner aliens, including ingested plants, animals, pharmaceuticals and the microbiomes upon which thinking itself relies'. Inhale. Exhale. Now, where did that urge for chocolate come from? Who decided to end this breathing exercise and run down to the street vender to fetch some chocolate? Influx. Efflux.

This strange feeling that emerges when we begin to notice how we are not confined, coherent subjects perfectly in control of our intentions, will, and actions is one of Bennett's most powerful analytical resources. If something comes out strongly throughout Bennett's writing, it is an ability to notice, marvel, be enchanted, and channel this enchantment into thinking and theorizing.

DOI: 10.4324/9781003182887-5

Throughout her work, Bennett strives to de-centre the human and recognize the agency of the other-than-human bodies with which we humans share the world. She carefully deconstructs the idea that human beings differ from all other creatures in their interpreting and self-interpreting capabilities. Bennett's insistent deconstruction of the idea of a confined, human being whose intentional actions causally effect the world can help organization studies to challenge the story of a sovereign self that continue to do its work in many debates in organization studies despite the fact that it has been subject of critique for quite some years (Harding, Gilmore and Ford, 2021; Pullen and Vachhani, 2013; Kenny and Fotaki, 2015; Ford et al., 2017; Pullen and Rhodes, 2015). Bennett's writing is an invitation to rework concepts such as will, intention, agency, (managerial) control and causality, seeing them not as the properties of individual bodies but as post-personal events in emerging confederations. Moreover, scholars of organization may find methodological inspiration not only in Bennett's original curiosity, but also in her careful manner of choosing words and creating languages better suited to theorise a world of vibrant matter and affective influences.

In this chapter, first, I introduce Bennett's seminal thinking on vibrant matter. Second, I present Bennett's ideas about affect and affective influences. Next, I describe the concepts of subjectivity and agency that comes out of Bennetts theorizing and discuss the possibilities these hold for organization theory and analysis. Finally, I unpack the methodological inspiration that Bennett's work offers and discuss how this may enrich organization studies.

Vibrant matter

With the concept of *vibrant matter* Bennett offers a decisive move away from thinking things as dead, dumb, brute, and passive matter that wait for humans to come along, notice and make use of them. She explores how edibles, commodities, storms, and metals sometime act as quasi agents with their own trajectories, potentialities, and tendencies (Bennett, 2010, p. viii). Such things, Bennett argues, are lively. The project is not to deny human agency or to release humans of their responsibility for how the world is developing. Rather, it is to discuss how the modern habit of parsing the world into passive matter and vibrant life has the effect that we often understate the power of things. What would happen if we think through the liveliness of matter, for example, how landfills generate lively streams of chemicals or the way a diet infiltrates brain chemistry and moods (Bennett, 2010a)? How can our analysis of organizations be enriched if we also direct our analytical attention to the creative self-organization of matter and its lively, inconsistent nature?

By dismissing the assumption that things or matter always behave in simple, mechanistic or predictable manners, Bennett offers theoretical and analytical sensitivity to how things sometimes demonstrate a curious ability to animate, to act and to produce dramatic and subtle effects (Bennett, 2010, p. 6). She is not arguing that the table I sit at while writing this chapter has intentions or a will. Rather, it is to explore what it would mean to admit that it has propensities and insistences. Bennett asks how different kinds of waste, chemicals, winds of methane or iron have certain tendencies, capacities and propulsions that sometime come to conjoin with other human and non-human bodies and thereby become powerful actants. The concept of actant comes from Bruno Latour and Bennett uses it to replace the concept of an actor. An actant is defined as 'an entity or a process that makes a difference to the direction of a larger assemblage without that difference being reducible to an efficient cause; actants collaborate, divert, vitalize, gum up, twist, or turn the groupings in which they participate' (Bennett in Watson, 2013, p. 149). This recast of things is a shift of focus not only from thinking things as passive entities waiting for humans to give them purpose, value and use, but also from thinking things in and of themselves (as, e.g. the part of new materialism working under the umbrella term *object oriented ontology* see Harman, 2011). Bennett's theory of vibrant matter is not about things as entities. Bennett's particular term, *thing power*, is not a concept for things in their individuality, stability and separateness. Rather, it is a concept that draws attention to the forces and intensities of things often in congregation with other human and non-human bodies. Of crucial importance here is the concept of assemblage. Imported primarily from the work of Deleuze and Guattari, Bennett uses this concept to stress how a phenomenon such as, for example, a breakdown of an electric power grid is in fact a network, a coming together, of many different things and forces that together have the capacity to disrupt as well as to generate actions and effects. Assemblages for Bennett mean:

> ad hoc groupings of diverse elements, of vibrant materials of all sorts. Assemblages are living, throbbing confederations that are able to function despite the persistent presence of energies that confound them from within. They have uneven topographies, because some of the points at which the various affects and bodies cross paths are move heavily trafficked than others, and so power is not distributed equally across its surface.
>
> (Bennett, 2010, pp. 23–24)

Assemblages are constantly changing and can be unpredictable and ungovernable. As Bennett writes:

> Assemblages are not governed by any central head: no one materiality or type of material has sufficient competence to determine consistently the trajectory or impact of the group. The effects generated by an assemblage are, rather, emergent properties, emergent in that their ability to make something happen (a newly inflected materialism, a blackout, a hurricane, a war on terror) is distinct from the sum of the vital force of each materiality considered alone. Each member and proto-member of the assemblage has a certain vital force, but there is also an effectivity proper to the grouping as such: an agency *of* the assemblage.
>
> (Bennett, 2010, p. 24)

Thus, against a tendency in scholarship and public discourses alike to often assume by default that the most potent actant in a group is a human being, Bennett draws attention to how complex networks escape human control and that inanimate things, like electronics or wind, can set off unintended consequences. This is important for attempts of organization scholars to discuss environmental issues: How are organizations part and parcel of large, complex and fundamentally ungovernable assemblages that often do harm to people, animals and ecosystems around the planet? Bennett's work resists any understanding of nature as passive and humans as the all-powerful actor that can bring nature to use. Instead, she offers possibilities to unpack how ideas about nature as inert resources fortifies organizations' exploitation of the planet.

New materialisms have already inspired organizational scholars to rethink concepts such as actor, identity and communication as well as relationships between the discursive and the material (Harding, 2020; Orlikowski, 2007; Orlikowski and Scott, 2015). Particularly, scholars have drawn on Karen Barad's agential realism to study the material dimensions of organising and subjectivity (Dale and Latham, 2015; Harding, Ford and Lee, 2017; Dille and Plotnikof, 2020). However, references to Bennett's work are scarcer. Corvellec (2019) has drawn on Bennett's notion of thing-power to develop an analytical approach to waste that allows scholars to read and question waste by letting themselves be interpellated by waste as a means to get to know it better. Moreover, Valtonen and Pullen (2021) take inspiration from Bennett (as well as other new materialist literature) to explore how stones affect thinking, being, and writing and how they may provoke new forms of responsibility towards the planet. Considering how rocks are lively, how they evolve, change and move, how they bring us in to contact with much larger temporalities, and how human bodies depend on minerals, Valtonen and Pullen develop an ethico-politics capable of recognising that humans cannot be separated out from vital materiality and that harming one member in the network, is also to harm others (Bennett, 2010, p. 13).

In times in which it is becoming more and more evident that plants, animals, ecosystems, minerals, fossil fuel and gases are not inert resources for organizational and private production and consumption, Bennett's work can push organization studies towards less human-centred thinking and a greater sensitivity to how all bodies – human and more-than human – are kin in inextricably enmeshed networks of relations. Ignorance of the lively powers of material formations is part and parcel of how harmful utilization and destruction of the planet continue. Recognizing that agency is not solely the province of humans might instead spur the cultivation of a more responsible, ecologically sound politics (Bennett, 2010, p. 14; Valtonen and Pullen, 2021).

Affect

Ideas about affect are omnipresent, indeed, a main influx and tonality in Bennett's work. The world she theorises is one of constant movement, a world of ebbs and flows of affect. A world, where moving around is to constantly affect and be affected by human and non-human forces. One example of how Bennett allows contemporary ideas of affect to bring about new appreciations of traditional concepts or phenomena is her reshaping of the notion of sympathy. In *Influx and efflux* (Bennett, 2020), by thinking with the writing of Whitman, Bennett stretches notions of influence, affection and sympathy 'beyond a human-centred, sentimental frame to include apersonal, underdetermined vital forces that course through selves without being reducible to them' (Bennett, 2020, p. xix). Bennett takes the notion of sympathy beyond a moral, social and psychological experience of a confined subject, and towards a more material and trans-subjective affective force. Sympathy here is not a psychological process whereby a subject projects her own pain or suffering on others, neither is it some form of imaginative identification. Instead, it is a 'more-than-human atmospheric force' (Bennett, 2020, p. 27). Sympathy is processes through which certain forces or allures come to feel heavy on the skin of a subject and pass through her pores to alter her in some ways, or more precisely alter what she is capable of doing (Bennett, 2020, p. 93). Sympathy comes to mean an affective tendency towards affiliation which is broader or more material than imaginative constructs. It is no longer an act or gesture of an individual that observes another human or animal, but a term that describes how bodies sometimes physically bend towards each other and a force by which one is affected or even 'possessed' (Whitman's term) by the circuits of pain, suffering, enthusiasm or excitement that one encounters and is enveloped by Bennett (2020, p. 31).

One of the potentials of thinking with Bennett's concept of sympathy is that it can allow us to transgress the hierarchies that often sneak their way into discourses and practices of diversity, charity or corporate ethics. In such discourses and practices, often, the sympathizer (the organization, the benefactor, the CEO etc.) is installed as the active subject that faces a passive object of pity (victims, minorities). Despite appealing ambitions of doing something good to help a minority, it can be difficult to escape this already-established and powerful hierarchy as long as sympathy and aid are thought through individualistic repertoires. As a consequence, powers of inequality may continue to flow through efforts to enhance equality (Ahmed, 2007; Benschop, 2001). As Blackmore (2006) has argued, when discourses of inclusion and diversity are framed through individualistic imperatives, the possibilities of delivering the promise of more inclusion and equality is quickly compromised as the source of agency and ethicality remains with the majority. The voices of minorities may be silenced or compromised with the same measures that were meant to give them a voice. Bennett's thinking opens possibilities of asking questions about diversity and organizational ethics with less dependence upon hierarchical relations between an active subject and the passive object of pity.

Leadership, agency and responsibility

Bennett's work with affect also offers an enrichment to discussions of leadership more broadly. Organizational scholars have criticized mainstream leadership theory for assuming leadership to be an individual, disembodied practice performed in cognitive and rational registers (Pullen and Vachhani, 2013; Kenny and Fotaki, 2015; Pullen and Rhodes, 2015; Ford et al., 2017; Ashcraft, 2021), noting that such narratives and theories rarely account for the collective, embodied, material, and practical aspects of leadership (Orr and Vince, 2009; Sinclair, 2013; Orr and Bennett, 2017). The concept of the individual that Bennett offers may help to bring such debates even further. The individual in Bennett's theoretical universe is not the one often found in management research and discourses, the one that is contained, rational and clearly separated from his environment: The centre from which agency and decision-making springs. Instead, the individual is a porous body capable of being affected by the environment in which she moves as well as of affecting that environment in direct and often not so direct manners. It is also an individual, which is thought via post-human theories. An individual, which is not only human but composed of human and non-human bodies and entangled to different human and non-human bodies and forces. Critical debates on management are offered a concept of the individual, not as an origin of initiatives and intentions. Bennett writes:

> No one body owns its supposedly own initiatives, for initiatives instantly conjoins with an impersonal swarm of contemporaneous endeavours, each with its own duration and intensity, with endeavours that are losing or gaining, rippling into and recombining with others.
>
> (Bennett 2010, p. 101)

In *Influx and efflux* Bennett finds in Whitman's writing a distinctive way of thinking about the individual. The term 'dividual' is used to emphasize that persons should not be thought to be individual, that is indivisible, bounded units. Bennett draws on Marriott (1976, p. iii) to think what it means to be a person: A 'dividual' absorb heterogenous material influences and 'give out themselves particles of their own substances' that may then 'reproduce in others something of the nature of the persons in whom they have originated' (Bennett, 2020, pp. xii–xiii). *Influx and Efflux* is one long meditation on what it means to be an I as the 'experience of being continuously subject to influence and still managing to add something to the mix' (xiii). Thus, the subject we find is a 'porous and susceptible shape that rides and imbibes waves of influx and efflux, but also contributes an "influence" of its own' (Bennett, 2020, p. xi).

For management and organization scholars striving to give yet another punch at the stubborn assumptions about individuality and individual agency in our discipline, this thinking offers a well-developed notion of the individual as something that is porous and entangled. It becomes possible to think about 'the leader' as a someone that does not pre-exist a range of different practices but emerges through entanglements to assemblages of things, objects, forces, bodies, norms and histories.

In organization studies, Ford et al. (2017) have built on ideas about matter as agentic and lively to unpack leadership as an emergent interplay between human and non-human bodies and forces. They argue that the leader cannot be understood separately and distinctively from her material presence, physical location, technology, clothes, accessories etc. This means that there is no leader who pre-exists leadership practices, as the long history of leadership theory has presumed. There is no simple notion of *the leader* to separate out as a single source of agency. Thus, the figure of a leader we find here lacks the assured autonomy and singular agency he often has in traditional management literature, yet this does not mean that a leader cannot make a difference. It is just not, as many leaders on the ground will recognize, with any direct causality, but better thought of as non-causal, and indirect manners of influencing. Bennett offers the concept of *partaking*, a notion that can emphasise how leadership is to be part of processes rather than in control of them. Change, then, is conceived as pluralized and distributed processes rather than being a matter of individual minds or agency (Taylor, 2017, p. 319).

Thus, against, ideas often found in traditional management literature about leadership as something that springs from the intentionality, and autonomy of individuals, Bennett's thinking offers an idea of leadership as the participation in assemblages where individuals participate but cannot initiate or direct. It offers attention to how leader subjectivity is the outcome of practices of partaking rather than something that can be isolated out and addressed as the source of change. Against mainstream leadership theories' fascination with how leaders can design and direct change, Bennett's thinking can help broaden considerably the analytical sensitivity to domains of unintended and unanticipated effects of leadership practices. This may help build more humble concepts of leadership, capable of appreciating the emergent, unpredictable and non-causal dimensions of leadership and organizational change (Ford et al., 2017; Pors, 2020).

Responsibility

It is important to discuss whether this deconstruction of the individual risks compromising accountability and responsibility. When we think about the leader as entangled to and emerging from complex assemblages what happens to the possibilities of holding people and organizations responsible and accountable to the harm they may produce? To acknowledge that it is not possible for one actor to control, oversee or manage the assemblages it is part of, should not serve as a tool for weakening and blurring discourses and devices working to hold human beings and organizations accountable for the damage production, they take active parts in. Bennett is very clear here: Recognizing that agency is distributed across mosaic assemblages does not and should not make it impossible to say something about the actions exercised by an organization within the assemblages it is part of, relies on and accelerates. Bennett writes:

> The notion of confederate agency does attenuate the blame game, but it does not thereby abandon the project of identifying (what

Arendt called) the sources of harmful effects. To the contrary, such a notion broadens the range of places to look for sources.

(Bennett, 2010, p. 37)

It remains important to make specific people and organizations accountable for their unjust, wrong, and illegal actions, and Bennett insists that her theorizing should be seen as a supplement to rather than a replacement of such efforts. The point is that we *also* need concepts of responsibility that does not fail in the face of complex assemblages. Contemporary organizations are part of very widespread and complex assemblages. Often, harm production is carefully outsourced. Because it is difficult to place responsibility in a complex world, we need a theory that focuses on entanglements and assemblages rather on the boundaries that separate individuals and organizations from their relations and networks (Visser and Davies, 2021). The concept of assemblage might help scholars of organization to problematize the boundaries contemporary organizations are so skilled at drawing between what is their responsibility and what they believe they cannot be held accountable for.

What to do in organizational analysis

Bennett's work can also be a source of methodological inspiration. Her work is an invitation to practice a form of research willing to linger in moments that seem strangely charged with affect or atmosphere although one may not at first be entirely sure what is at stake or what one might learn from such moments. It is an invitation to slow down time and let oneself be enchanted by the richness of even mundane settings or events. Bennett asks those interested in vibrant matters to 'linger in those moments during which they find themselves fascinated by objects' (2010, p. 17) so that the affective force of what is apprehended can be felt.

There is a rich methodological tradition of dwelling in *small* moments or encounters in an extensive data collection/production process in organization studies. Moving beyond methodological norms of representation scholars have argued for a manner of working with data where the researcher dwells in what may at first seem like a minor or fleeting occurrence (Kociatkiewicz and Kostera, 1999; Gherardi, 2019; Pors, 2016). Deleuze and Guattari writes about the power of 'the little detail that starts to swell and carries you off' (1986, p. 292, cited in Bennett, 2020, p. 68). To dwell in one particular encounter or moment involves work to carefully unpack the affective qualities of the moment, consider its textures, multiplicity and layers, as well as to thoroughly and creatively assemble the forces, lines, vibrant agencies and histories that seem to encounter each other in such a moment (Bell and Vachhani, 2020; Edensor, 2020).

The methodological question then becomes: When doing fieldwork, how do we take in and allow ourselves to be profoundly influenced by the moments, forces, people and things we encounter? What are our methodological strategies for dwelling in and concern ourselves with particular, perhaps minor, moments that seem saturated with meaning and intensity, although the researcher is at first not exactly sure why? Following the impetus in Bennett's work, a central methodological skill becomes the ability of the researcher to be surprised, perhaps even enchanted, or spooked (Pors, 2021), by the things she may meet in the world around her (Bennett, 2001). In her reading of Whitman, Bennett returns several times to this phrase: 'The scene and all its belongings, how they seize and affect me' (Whitman in Bennett, 2020, e.g. p. 67). When we enter organizations, when we encounter certain moments, events, people, things, and assemblages how do we allow ourselves to be seized and affected? How do we notice and become influenced by the different forces, bodies, relations, things, ideas and discourses that belong to a scene?

Although this form of thinking and writing rest upon the ability of the researcher to dwell in, feel and let herself be enchanted by the affective forces encountered, the idea is not that the researcher can never be a neutral, or passive medium in which certain truths about the field can be imprinted. The researcher is present in certain settings with specific theoretical interests, disciplinary training, capacities, histories and inclinations for noticing certain things. There is always something that guides us when we encounter an empirical setting. How can Bennett's analytical strategy guiding her interests and attentions be described?

To sharpen her ability to be surprised, Bennett finds inspirations in Henry David Thoreau's notion of *the wild* and how this incites a noticing of the surprise, excess or errancy simmering within ordinary objects capable of disrupting our habits of perception and derail trains of thoughts (Bennett, 2020, p. 90). More specifically, perhaps, Bennett lets her attentions be guided by an interest in things that might be left out of certain dominant narratives (for example of disenchantment, Bennett, 2001, or of matter as inert, Bennett, 2010). Bennett calls this strategy 'trash collection':

> I am less its [disenchantments] critic than its trash collector. . .. I dust off and shine up what it discards, that is, experiences of wonder and surprise that endure alongside a cynical world of business as usual, nature as manmade and affects as the effects of commercial strategy.

The experiences that I recycle, . . . are not invaders of the major tale but underground and background of it.

(Bennett, 2001, p. 8)

To be a trash collector is a particular analytical strategy involving efforts to identify the ideas, assumptions, possibilities, phenomena, things, ways of being that are left out or rubbished by the narratives and discourses that dominate certain sites, organizations, or fields. The project is not necessarily to prove wrong and replace particular powerful narratives, but rather to add to them other and alternative stories. It is to pick up those things that (no longer) holds a place in contemporary thinking and make small spaces, where one can stay with them, allow them to grow and mature until alter stories can emerge. This is an analytical strategy that works by amplifying and putting in motion that what is already there in different scenes or accounts, but which is normally not granted attention or considered as agentic (Blackman, 2019). In the context of organizational analysis: If we usually assume that resistance to organizational change is done by people, what might we learn by also considering the influence of material, non-sentient actors or of uncanny affective atmospheres (Harding, Ford and Lee, 2017; Pors, 2016)? It also means that the researcher directs her attention to those things that escape or do not fit our usual categories – to those things that exceed present languages and assumptions (Pors, Olaison and Otto, 2019). What kinds of forces and agencies are not considered with established concepts of leadership and what interesting and important stories could be told by picking up what is expelled and rubbished from these concepts?

The strategy of trach collection involves careful consideration of how to write. As Bennett (2020, p. xxi) notes, the challenge is how to place affects and vibrant matter in a language and normative scientific milieu that is not their home. Sometimes, Bennett suggests, the researcher needs to be willing to appear to be a bit naïve. To consider and make space for affect or vibrant matter in academic texts, it may be fruitful to get a little bit closer to animism, anthropomorphism, vitalism and superstition than what may feel comfortable in a world where such things are now associated with premodernity (Bennett, 2010, p. 18). It is difficult, but also promising to constantly and carefully notice how languages accommodate and give a further life to certain assumptions, for example assumptions about autonomous individuality or differences between human beings and all other creatures and things in the world. Bennett's work generously offers a number of 'workarounds to the grammar of subjects and object' (Bennett, 2020, p. xxiv). Bennett calls this craft 'writing up' and explains this as efforts to amplify, inflect or tilt what is already underway although it may not be the most obvious story of an empirical setting or event (Bennett, 2020, p. 112). For organization scholars, this is as invitation to consider whether we have the right words and concepts for the complexities we are studying. If we believe leadership is not only performed by individuals but also achieved by practices, assemblages and materiality, which words and concepts become difficult because they sneak back in assumptions about individuality? And which words and concepts may better capture the multiple processes and assemblages that together produces agency?

Bennett's discussion about writing up is an important reminder that we might not be able to genuinely foster new, more eco-sensitive and responsible thinking and research without critically considering the languages, concepts, methodologies and styles of writing we are trained to work with and within. There is work to be done in terms of experimenting with and inventing new forms of thinking and writing. This includes the collective work of challenging and changing a scientific milieu where clear findings, unambivalent conclusions and a distinct and unmistakable contribution to the literature often equals quality.

Conclusion

Breath in the wonders of the world in which you find yourselves and to which you are entangled. Reflect for a moment upon the different epistemological constructions at work around you that stubbornly assumes that the confined human individual is the only source of agency, and that plants, minerals, plastic, woods and electricity are objects of human interventions. Breath out. What manners of thinking differently about subject-object relations and causality may be available to you?

Thinking with Bennett is not only about understanding her original definitions of concepts. It is about breathing wonder into the things, relations and forms of organising you thought you knew so that once again they seem curious and mysterious. So that they once again ask you to think carefully about organising, identity, leadership and organizational ethics. In his engagement with Freud, Derrida (1995, p. 26) calls this a process that allows and make possible that texts, figures or images – through efforts to get to know them – become 'secret, young and still to come'. The aim of Bennett's explorative endeavour is not to resolve or settle certain doubts or ambivalences, but be able to accommodate, even amplify the complexity and uncertainty of the material one is working with. Her concepts and writing are meant to carefully twist things around so that the individual is no longer as autonomous and confined as we sometimes tend to think. They are meant to help us open our eyes to how the things we have been taught are passive inert things, actually have tendencies, propensities and inclinations of their own.

Doing organizational analysis in the company of Bennett's ideas requires an attention to how there are always more forces, agencies, and relations at work than what we first assume. It also requires us to consider whether our concepts, analytical approaches and conclusions are 'roomy enough to accommodate a heterogeneous swirl of agents, some human' (Bennett, 2020, p. xxiv). Her thinking begins with the strange experience that we are not confined, coherent subjects perfectly in control of our intentions, will and actions. It takes us on a journey to discover the liveliness, agencies and forces of things we thought were inert and dead. And, possibly, if we allow it to, it leaves us transformed by the realization that we are connected to the world around us in profound and existential ways. Inhale. Exhale. Let yourself be enchanted!

Note

1   *Influx and efflux* is the title of Jane Bennett's book from 2020 that seeks and finds in Walt Whitman's writing a distinctive idea of the subject, of what it means to be a person. The book invites and invokes a thinking that is embodied and in flux. The ideas of the book, and, perhaps, of Bennett's other important work too, is best understood if one allows thinking and breathing to accompany each other.

Recommended reading

Original text by Jane Bennett

Bennett, J. (2010). *Vibrant matter. A political ecology of things.* Durham: Duke University Press.

Key academic text

Taylor, C.A. (2017). Rethinking the empirical in higher education: Post-qualitative inquiry as a less comfortable social science. *International Journal of Research & Method in Education*, 40(3), pp. 311–324.

Accessible resource

Watson, J. (2013). Eco-sensibilities: An interview with Jane Bennett. *The Minnesota Review*, 2013(81), pp. 147–158. Available at: https://muse.jhu.edu/article/526431/pdf?casa_token=fpzrJmkAZI8AAAAA:Om57rRFheP2IGDAuUL-F2nyWdUE rphrOCkvtDcVPLfRNYaFIARTOeCRKz0ZyyDHtyNF5e9Ojhds

References

Ahmed, S. (2007). The language of diversity. *Ethnic and Racial Studies*, 30(2), pp. 235–256.

Ashcraft, K. (2021). Communication as constitutive transmission? An encounter with affect. *Communication Theory*, 31(4), pp. 571–592.

Bell, E. and Vachhani, S.J. (2020). Relational encounters and vital materiality in the practice of craft work. *Organization Studies*, 41(5), pp. 681–701.

Bennett, J. (2001). *The enchantment of modern life*. Princeton: Princeton University Press.

Bennett, J. (2010). *Vibrant matter*. Durham: Duke University Press.

Bennett, J. (2020). *Influx and efflux*. Durham: Duke University Press.

Benschop, Y. (2001). Pride, prejudice and performance: Relations between HRM, diversity and performance. *International Journal of Human Resource Management*, 12(7), pp. 1166–1181.

Blackman, L. (2019). *Haunted data: Affect, transmedia and weird science*. London: Bloomsbury.

Blackmore, J. (2006). Deconstructing diversity discourses in the field of educational management and leadership. *Educational Management Administration & Leadership*, 34(2), pp. 181–199.

Corvellec, H. (2019). Waste as scats: For an organizational engagement with waste. *Organization*, 26(2), pp. 217–235.

Dale, K. and Latham, Y. (2015). Ethics and entangled embodiment: Bodies – materialities – organization. *Organization*, 22(2), pp. 166–182.

Derrida, J. (1995). *Archive Fever: A Freudian impression*. Chicago: University of Chicago Press.

Dille, M. and Plotnikof, M. (2020). Retooling methods for approaching discourse – materiality relations: A new materialist framework of multimodal sensitivity. *Qualitative Research in Organizations and Management: An International Journal*, 15(4), pp. 485–501.

Edensor, T. (2020). *Stone: Stories of urban materiality*. Manchester: Springer Nature.

Felix, G., & Guattari, D. (1986). *A thousand plateaus: Capitalism and schizophrenia*. Trans. by Massumi, B.). Minneapolis: University of Minnesota.

Ford, J., Harding, N. Gilmore, S. and Richardson, S. (2017). Becoming the leader: Leadership as material presence. *Organization Studies*, 38(11), pp. 1553–1571.

Gherardi, S. (2019). Theorizing affective ethnography for organization studies. *Organization*, 26(6), pp. 741–760.

Harding, N. (2020). Materialities and identities. In: A. Brown, ed., *The Oxford Handbook of Identities in Organizations*. Oxford: Oxford University Press.

Harding, N., Ford, J. and Lee, H. (2017). Towards a performative theory of resistance: Senior managers and revolting subject (ivitie) s. *Organization Studies*, 38(9), pp. 1209–1232.

Harding, N., Gilmore, S. and Ford, J. (2021). Matter that embodies: Agentive flesh and working bodies/selves. *Organization Studies*. doi:10.1177/0170840621993235.

Harman, G. (2011). *The quadruple object*. London. Zero Books.

Kenny, K. and Fotaki, M. (2015). From gendered organizations to compassionate borderspaces: Reading corporeal ethics with Bracha Ettinger. *Organization*, 22(2), pp. 183–199.

Kociatkiewicz, J., & Kostera, M. (1999). *The anthropology of empty spaces*. Qualitative Sociology, 22, pp. 37–50.

Marriott, M. (1976). *Interpreting Indian society: A monistic alternative to Dumont's dualism*. The Journal of Asian Studies, 36(1), pp. 189–195.

Orlikowski, W. (2007). Sociomaterial practices: Exploring technology at work. *Organization Studies*, 28(9), pp. 1435–1448.

Orlikowski, W. and Scott, S. (2015). Exploring material-discursive practices. *Journal of Management Studies*, 52(5), pp. 697–705.

Orr, K. and Bennett, M. (2017). Relational leadership, storytelling, and narratives: Practices of local government chief executives. *Public Administration Review*, 77(4), pp. 515–527.

Orr, K. and Vince, R. (2009). Traditions of local government. *Public Administration*, 87(3), pp. 655–677.

Pors, J. (2016). 'It sends a cold shiver down my spine': Ghostly interruptions to strategy implementation. *Organization Studies*, 37(11), pp. 1641–1659.

Pors, J. (2020). Local meaning-making in discursive, embodied and affective registers. *International Journal of Public Leadership*, 17(3), pp. 247–264.

Pors, J. (2021). A ghostly encounter and the questions we might learn from it. *Culture and Organization*, 27(4), pp. 289–301.

Pors, J., Olaison, L. and Otto, B. (2019). Ghostly matters in organizing. *Ephemera Theory and Politics in Organization*, 19(1), pp. 1–29.

Pullen, A. and Rhodes, C. (2015). Ethics, embodiment and organizations. *Organization*, 22(2), pp. 159–165.

Pullen, A. and Vachhani, S. (2013). The materiality of leadership. *Leadership*, 9(3), pp. 315–319.

Sender, R., Fuchs, S. and Milo, R. (2016). Revised estimates for the number of human and bacteria cells in the body. *PLoS Biology*, 14(8), p. e1002533. https://doi.org/10.1371/journal.pbio.1002533.

Sinclair, A. (2013). A material dean. *Leadership*, 9, pp. 436–443.

Taylor, C. (2017). Rethinking the empirical in higher education: Post-qualitative inquiry as a less comfortable social science. *International Journal of Research & Method in Education*, 40(3), pp. 311–324.

Valtonen, A. and Pullen, A. (2021). Writing with rocks. *Gender, Work and Organization*, 28(2), pp. 506–522.

Visser, L. and Davies, O. (2021). The becoming of online healthcare through entangled power and performativity: A posthumanist agential realist perspective. *Organization Studies*, 42(12), pp. 1817–1837.

Watson, J. (2013). Eco-sensibilities: An interview with Jane Bennett. *The Minnesota Review*, 2013(81), pp. 147–158.

6 Becoming With Barad

A Material-Discursive-Affective Conversation

Noortje van Amsterdam, Katrine Meldgaard Kjær and Dide van Eck

Dear Reader,

In this chapter, we discuss the relationship between Karen Barad's works and the theme of affect in Management and Organization Studies (MOS). Providing new opportunities to understand material agencies, Barad's feminist new materialist ideas have been first adopted in MOS to understand the use of technology in organizations (e.g. Dale and Latham, 2015; Nyberg, 2009; Orlikowski, 2007; Orlikowski and Scott, 2015a, 2015b; Symon and Pritchard, 2015). More recently, MOS scholars have been using Barad's work to come to a relational understanding of the sociomateriality of, for example, leadership (Ford et al., 2017), gendered embodiment (Harding et al., 2017, 2022), craft (Bell and Vachhani, 2020), disability (Dale and Latham, 2015; Bend and Priola, 2021), sexual violence (Harris, McFarlane and Wieskamp, 2020), digital healthcare (Visser & Davies, 2021), the co-existence of people with animals (Huopalainen, 2020) and the natural environment (Valtonen and Pullen, 2020).

The turn to affect in MOS can be considered part of a larger shift in ontological orientations that is marked by a movement away from anthropocentrism, focusing instead on relationality (Gherardi, 2017, 2019). Although Barad's work centralizes relationality, the relationship between their theorizing and affect is not straightforward. As Ringrose, Warfield and Zarabadi (2020) write "affect is given hardly any attention in some posthuman accounts such as Barad" (p. 12). This leaves open the obvious question of why Barad's work belongs in a volume on affect in organization studies, as well as the challenge of bringing into view this relationship. Nonetheless, we enthusiastically accepted the invitation to write this chapter, not because we consider ourselves authorities on Barad's work, but because we are intrigued by the question of affect in relation to it and want to learn more. We were also excited to work collaboratively on this: over the past years we have created a supportive feminist community

DOI: 10.4324/9781003182887-6

in which we publish and related to each other through care and vulner-ability (e.g. Meldgaard-Kjær and van Amsterdam, 2020; van Eck, van Amsterdam and van den Brink, 2021). Some of this work also engages with Barad's theorizing (van Amsterdam, Meldgaard Kjær and van Eck, 2022). In this chapter, we build on our previous engagements by offering not an authoritative account of the complex relationship between Barad, affect and MOS, but instead showing how these may come together in the practice of writing this chapter collaboratively. We will offer our insights through a conversation between us – Noortje, Katrine and Dide – combined with three textboxes that explain some of Barad's most important concepts. These concepts are marked with a ★ in the text, so you know where you are reading a concept from Barad that is defined and unpacked in a textbox. The conversation unfolds through the intra-action★ between the authors, Barad's texts, computer screens, warm tea, pets, the publication process, the COVID-19 pandemic, google scholar, our work/home spaces, other writings on new materialism within MOS, and much more. In this chapter, we engage with the idea of affect as the felt intensities produced by the encounter of us writers with the world around us. We illustrate the relationship between affect and Barad's work diffractively★, as we are reading it through our experiences and the mate-rial realities these are wrapped up with, showcasing the affective flows that are produced. Each email evokes a response and we come to know ourselves and each other differently/anew through this process.

Barad coins the concept **"intra-action"** as "the constitution of **entangled** agencies" (2007, p. 31), referring to the inextricability of discourses and human and non-human materialities that together co-produce realities in particular times and spaces: "[a]ll bodies, not merely 'human' bodies, come to matter through the world's itera-tive intra-activity" (2003, p. 82). Agency here is thus not the exclu-sive property of a singular actor, but rather arises in intra-actions between discourses and materialities, including human and non-human bodies. This is fundamental to Barad's larger framework of **agential realism** (1999, 2003, 2007) that posits that human actors are not singular or autonomous subjects, but entangled with (non-)human materialities such as objects, nature and spaces. Affect, however, is rarely mentioned explicitly by Barad. Accord-ing to Ashcraft (2020, p. 3), affect, "a potentiality or agency in motion", is produced through intra-actions, but at the same time, affect "by definition, repels definition" (ibid.). The link between affect and Barad's theory on materiality in MOS surfaces mostly in work drawing on practice theory (e.g. Bell and Vachhani, 2020; Gherardi, 2017, 2019; Gherardi et al., 2018).

★★★

Hi both,

How are you? Surviving the increasing craziness of the pandemic OK? It seems like we are in a partial lockdown here again due to rapidly rising COVID cases. Pfff, luckily we can still go outside.

I have been thinking about our chapter on Barad for the collection on affect in MOS. I was wondering if we could do this in the format of a conversation where we not only discuss the theory but also relate our understanding of it to each other, the situation of the pandemic that we are currently facing and the human and non-human materialities that are structuring our work at the moment (such as kids/partners/pets at home, online interfaces, laptops, food, drinks, literature, a VIRUS, home office struggles etc). I thought it might be a nice way of showing the 'becoming' of the chapter while adhering to the theoretical principles of intra-action★, diffraction★, and ethics★.

I would love to hear what you think!

Hugs

★★★

Hi both,

At the moment I am also slowly digesting yesterday's news of the partial lockdown and the fact that we are now one of the hardest hit countries in terms of COVID-19 infections – I feel like my brain is blocking me from understanding this situation fully. At the same time I feel lucky that I can continue working from home. Also, I am constantly checking my email for any responses on my application for a tenure-track position and feel tense every time I hear the 'new-email' ping of my computer – no response so far.

I like your idea. This format of a conversation would, I think, better allow us to do justice to Barad's ethico-onto-epistemology (2007, p. 90); rather than writing our chapter as a linear and static set of ideas we can show through our conversation how producing academic knowledge is a situated and relational practice that carries the ethical imperative of being accountable to the world itself and its human and non-human inhabitants. The only thing I worry about, I have to admit, is that "my voice" will not sound as smart as your voices. In this format it becomes more visible who says what compared to a conventional collaborative format.

In practical terms: shall we create a google doc that allow us all to contribute or do you want to keep it as an email conversation?

Hugs

★★★

Barad (2007, p. 30) proposes **diffraction** as an alternative to reflection that "does not fix what is object and what is subject in advance" but instead involves "reading insights through one another in ways that help illuminate differences as they emerge: how different differences get made, what gets excluded, and how these exclusions matter". Barad explains this using the metaphor of waves (2014): If you drop a stone in water, it creates a particular rippling effect. If you then drop another stone in the water (or a twig for that matter) the rippling effects of both plunges meet up and form an "interference pattern" that brings new details into view (2007, p. 71). Diffraction is thus a relational process that destabilizes seemingly fixed boundaries and produces new realities through intra-action, including affective intensities. Harris, McFarlane and Wieskamp (2020) provide an example of how diffraction may be used in MOS. They show how the concept helps to expose the systemic nature of sexual harassment and the deflection of responsibility by organizations. Rather than looking at high-profile incidents of sexual harassment separately, "as if they were stones", they drew the impact of these incidents together diffractively, "at the point where these concentric circles of ripples meet" (Harris, McFarlane and Wieskamp, 2020, pp. 664–445).

Dear both,

I think it sounds like a wonderful idea, I'm in!

I find it interesting that the issue of (academic) shame and exposure comes up right away – especially in a piece about affect and organization. Of course you are every bit as qualified and smart as us and I would relish the opportunity to write with you! Shame as an affect seems so ingrained in academic practice – I certainly often feel it. Why is shame so central still? Is it produced through the intra-action★ of neoliberalization and discourses on competition in academia? What/who else is involved? Whose service is it in?

I hope we can do something with this piece that tries to counteract the shame often involved in academic work which is an ethical impera-tive indeed! Can we start by doing away with the individualization in our writing? If we take Barad's (2003, 2007) ideas around entanglements★ seriously, I would say that our individuality as authors is untenable. Barad acknowledges this when they write about the others such as friends, aca-demic disciplines and beaches that were entangled★ in writing Meeting the Universe Halfway (2007, p. x). Maybe we should not portray our-selves as Noortje, Dide or Katrine, but as a flow of voices and thinking that diffractively★ develop ideas.

As for COVID, I am sorry to hear about the lockdown. I saw yesterday that France was also closing down again. In contrast, as I was getting on the train this morning, I forgot to put on a mask. Masks are mandatory in public transportation here and have been for a while. But I was thinking about something else and simply . . . forgot. How freeing and privileged. At the same time, restaurants and bars, cafes, and places of gathering are now mandated to close at 10 pm, and I have been working from home for the last month due to restrictions that just seem to continue indefi-nitely. Teaching still goes on partially on campus. To me, everything is a mess of openings and closings. Of moments of forgetting and fretting, of worry and apathy. With Barad, I would say that these experiences emerge through the entanglement★ of all agencies described above. Change feels imminent.

Hugs!

★★★

Hi both,

I am super excited that you are both happy with the idea of diffractive★ writing apart-together for the chapter on Barad. I am very much look-ing forward to collaborating with you on this!! I feel lucky to be in the company of such amazingly smart and supportive women. I understand and relate to your feelings of shame and fear of exposure (hello imposter syndrome) but from my perspective they are not warranted at all. Let's indeed see how we can try to undo them in this writing. I am all for your suggestion of de-individualizing the conversation, and showcasing the unfolding of this book chapter.

I think these issues very much intra-act★ with ideas and practices around authorship. Indeed, if we are true to Barad's theorizing, and see everything as entangled*, then claiming authorship on writing that is always already informed by previous conversations, experiences and readings (to name but a few) does not make any sense, does it? Other collective writings have argued this as well (e.g. Davies and Gannon, 2012)

Yet within academia the metrics system is entangled* with authorship and authority claims. The affect (in terms of what this produces) is shameful subjects. As Jones et al. (2020, p. 369) write, the quantification of academic research reduces human subjects to objects, leads to competition among academics and creates a closed, anxious and defensive working climate. And since this phenomenon also includes gendered elements, shame is more heavily felt for women in academia. Indeed, research supports this (e.g. Breeze, 2018; Moore, 2018).

Hugs!

★★★

Reading your emails is a nice start of the week ☺. I will take some days off this week – to walk, read, be outside, and do other stuff than work (within what is allowed in our partial lockdown).

Thank you for your reflections and understanding of my insecurities in individualizing our contributions to the chapter. It is really helpful to 'explain' how this affect/feeling is produced as you mentioned, through the intra-action* of gender constructions, the neoliberalization of the university, metrics etc. Yet although I can somewhat rationally explain how this is produced – I still cannot get rid of the feelings of shame and insecurity. I feel I need to re-engage with the ideas of Karen Barad on 'affect' to be able to contribute to this conversation. I therefore re-read an article by Bell and Vachhani (2020), who, building on Barad (2007), propose an *affective* ethics* of mattering that "acknowledges the vitality of matter and its affective capacities, and shows how matter comes to matter through embodied organizational practice" (p. 18).

The emphasis on **ethics** and **responsibility** is crucial in Barad's work. According to Barad (2010, p. 265), "entanglements are relations of obligation" and because we, as people and as researchers, co-produce these entanglements we cannot position ourselves as innocent bystanders but instead are ethically obliged to respond to human and non-human others. The methodology of diffraction, for Barad (in Juelskjær and Schwennesen, 2012, p. 16), makes this ethical **response-ability** possible because it entails an "ethico-onto-epistemological engagement, attending to differences and matters of care in all their detail in order to creatively re-pattern world-making practices with an eye to our indebtedness to the past and the future". Although Barad does not mention 'affect' explicitly here, their concern for the capacity to affect and be affected by the world comes through in the way they conceptualized ethics, responsibility, and care. They write that "there is no getting away from ethics" and emphasize the need to "take responsibility for the role that we play in the world's differential becoming" (2007, p. 396). As such, Barad is concerned with entanglements, and, as Bell and Vachhani (2020) add, their affective capacities we co-produce in organizational practice and research.

While trying to write to you about Barad's ideas on the affective capacities of non-human matter, my cat jumped on my lap to stop me from typing or using the computer mouse (see attachments, and yes I am wearing my chill-pants and a soft blanket). His comforting presence while struggling to understand Barad's ideas reminds me of human–animal relatedness that Huopalainen (2020) argues has the capability to "engage differently with the sensate, more-than-human life-worlds that humancentred accounts of organizational life have typically sentimentalised, trivialised or overlooked" (p. 1).

It also made me think of the vitality of the matter of a computer and e-mail that is co-constituting our conversation. On the one hand, through this conversation we try to better "account[ing] for our part of the entangled★ webs we weave" (Barad, 2008, p. 335) by showing how 'knowledge' emerges through our conversations during the pandemic. At the same time, our online exchange forestalls embodied encounters, being able to feel each other's presence. And, in terms of temporality, the conversation is asynchronous. I like how it allows us some time to think before responding to what others are saying (I often get blocked when I have to respond immediately in academic debates), and engage with the ideas during a moment that suits us best. Yet we also have to be careful about feeling pressured to respond quickly.

What do you think about our particular writing style and format in drawing out the affective intensities of reading/discussing/writing Barad's work collaboratively?

Hugs!

★★★

Image 6.1 E-mail attachment

I think we should make your cat co-author!
★★★

I also like having this conversation in my inbox, it feels like it becomes a more natural part of my day and as though we are having an actual conversation, somehow. Thinking about materiality, it's like I have you both with me when you pop up in my mailbox – maybe because I have a habit of checking and writing email on my phone (as I am doing now), and thus bring you with me in this way to my morning coffee on the couch, on my trips to the supermarket, on my commute (as long as we are still allowed to commute), to the office, and now to my living room once again. I often think it's a bad habit to do this phone-emailing, but there's a special kind of intimacy in it which I quite like and which brings it into intra-action★ with something else than the regular office. Things come out of that I can't quite account for but which feel joyful.

There's also something about the temporality of answering email that seems like something I can actually DO. I'm noticing my mood swings a lot right now and that I feel easily defeated and overwhelmed – I guess

I am affectively produced as such by the entangled★ agencies of the pandemic and everything/everyone else in my life. Opening a document can feel like opening another project that I feel overwhelmed by. No doubt this is because I am preoccupied by everything that's going on. In the midst of COVID, we are also experiencing another wave here: what people are calling a "second wave" of #metoo, with major press attention being directed towards sexism in all kinds of businesses, and currently culminating in two prominent politicians stepping down in the space of not very many days due to harassment issues previously kept silent. It's making me wonder what other kinds of action COVID is participating in making space for, and why. Maybe it's something about being pushed to the edge by all matter of things – and then finally reacting and becoming fed up.

★★★

Hi both,

Thanks for your messages. I love how we have become part of your morning coffee and other everyday activities with this conversation! It really feels joyful to work together on the chapter in this way. Yesterday I was trying to formulate a more in-depth response about Barad's (2008) work on queer causation. I started to read the text, but I got super frustrated. I felt like I was ploughing through pages and pages of ideas about biology, brittlestars, mimicry and cloning and all I could think was 'Get to the point, Karen! I have 5 more papers to write; 2 courses to teach; 4 reviews to complete; 2 PhDs to supervise; 2 online meetings with colleagues to prepare; 2 papers to revise; 1 master theses student to uplift, who seems to have gotten stuck in a depressive episode partly due to COVID; there is a total lockdown looming; my daughter keeps shouting from her room that she needs help with her homework; and the laundry is threatening to overtake my workspace/bedroom. I DON'T HAVE TIME TO READ THESE ENDLESS EPISTLES THAT I DON'T READILY UNDERSTAND'. So then I felt ashamed (there we are again) for apparently not understanding what other people do seem to grasp. Why did I think I could write a chapter on Barad's theorizing?? And I also felt guilty for not engaging with this text more, or others who use Barad's work. So that is me at the moment, feeling a bit overwhelmed and anxious.

I know there are different becomings possible than this frustrated and anxious one – for example, when I feel intrigued by Barads theorizing and this makes me eager to understand, when I read her interviews (e.g. Juelskjær and Schwennesen, 2012), and when we relate to their theorizing together in ways that are characterized by care, kindness and generosity. Although Barad writes about ethics★ I don't always feel cared for as a reader of their work. I just had to get that off my chest. Does that resonate at all?

Hugs!

★★★

Dear both,

I recognize what you are saying about only understanding theoretical ideas in a rational/intellectual way, and not *feeling* it in an embodied way. This is perhaps also what we sometimes run up against when reading Barad's work? That it is too much oriented on the mind and not connecting to the body, caring for the reader to help understand/feel/experience their agential realist★ framework? How could we engage the reader affectively and in an embodied way in this chapter?

★★★

Thank you for your reflections on Barad and embodiment. It's interesting because their focus on materiality to me very much calls for a focus on the body, in particular its non-verbal agencies; as Barad argues in a critique of poststructural analysis in her article Posthumanist Performativity (2003), "it is hard to deny that the power of language has been substantial . . . too substantial" (p. 802) and that the material now needs to have more focus. This also opens the door for using their work to think about the experiences you describe, as not only personal reactions but co-constructive elements of a process of things becoming. Barad would argue that there is an ethical obligation to be respons-able★, a term I would argue they use to draw our attention to the obligation to be attentive and respond to what is already there in our analyses, to the embodied and how our bodies react.

★★★

Hello awesome women,

How are you doing? Are you able to cope with the anxieties brought on by the second pandemic wave and related measures? I long for the physical proximity of friends, just to be able to hug and touch them/you and be near them/you without thinking of the health risks involved. Last week, I hit a rough patch too and had to take a few days off work. As you know, the mouth mask regulations are a problem for me and after two weeks of trying to manage/ignore increased flashbacks and hypervigilance, it felt like my body just sort of started to break down – I was a mess of nausea, headaches, stomach cramps, shaking hands and hyperventilation. Talk about how the intra-action★ between non-human materialities (a virus, mouth masks) and human materiality (my trauma-tized body) performs me in particular ways!! Taking a few days off helped to get back to tolerable levels of stress, but I need a long-term strategy to deal with this. It's work in progress, I guess. But I have to say, conversa-tions like the one we are having here keep me afloat. They make me feel connected and cared for. So thank you!! Caring collaborations are indeed a (feminist) strategy for survival.

I have been reading a great article today by Staunæs and Brøgger (2020). They write about metrics and the ways in which these are used in academia as mechanisms for monitoring and self-governance. They use a feminist new materialist lens to show how metric data – through their entanglement★ with other human and non-human agencies in academia – produce particular affective economies related to shame and envy. It showcases how Barad's theorizing informs thinking about affect, for example when they write about the per-formativity of data:

> Data may affect us in different ways, and the affects resulting from this may vary. An analytical approach towards the thing-power of data must, therefore, enable us to grasp the affective energy as flow-ing activity, as well as a pattern in which affects are composed, fig-ured, entangled★, mobilised and recruited.

> (p. 5)

Last thing I really like about this paper is that it writes about affirmative critique. With a group of 30 PhD students they experimented with the idea of reconceptualizing academic value otherwise. Staunæs and Brøgger employ the concepts of care and collaboration as response-able ethics★, and I think this is at the core of the feminist supportive writing practices we have going here as well. They reference Barad (2012, p. 7) too: "Each of us is constituted as responsible for the other, as being in touch with the other" in order to argue that their practices of imagining academic value differently "enable another set of senses than the visual, and how they succeed in 'bringing home affective energy' to the academics rather than producing malign affects" (p. 11).

I am curious to hear your thoughts on this. How can this help us to move towards other (more caring) academic practices and value systems? Does this only work in/from the margins or do you see possibilities for wider applications? How can we escape the push and pull of the metrics that produce us in these undesirable ways?

Hugs!!!

★★★

Hi both,

Thanks for sharing Staunæs and Brøgger's recent work. Surely, a change in mentality towards response-able ethics★ would require a complete reworking of academic practice and academic writing; writing differently and collaboratively and with vulnerability, as we are in the midst of right here, is a radical step in that direction. I think *what* we write and *how* we write is inherently material and relational too. We cannot separate the ways words materialize and are structured – the writing style and format – from their 'content'; there is a discursive-material entanglement★ in that. Indeed, the materiality of the structure of traditional academic writing co-constructs the performance of 'scholarship'. The often very emotionally charged reactions and disapproval you can encounter when challenging this format is indicative of how affect is a part of this entanglement★: the specific material-discursive performance of scholarship here also involves a sense of security and a disruption of that provokes uncertainty and unease; can this *really* be scholarship if it doesn't take the material form we know?

Hugs!

★★★

Hi both,

How are you both holding up with the general pressures of life on top of all the COVID measures and related insecurities? Shall we do a skype meeting soon? Although I really love this asynchronous conversation, I miss seeing you both!!!

I think what you write about the material-discursive performance of scholarship is very on point. The pushback against other forms of writing/thinking/doing in academia can be fierce and indeed shows how affect is wrapped up in these entanglements★ as we have all experienced with some of our publications. There can be resentment, anger even (which I often read as based on fear) in response to these different academic practices, but also encouragement and solidarity (see also Mandalaki and Péretz, 2021). I wonder what allows us to become differently here, in spite of the traditional structures typically favoured in academia. Is it the way we build upon scholars such as Barad who have provided new openings for scholarly practices? Or is it because we know this different performance of scholarship is often welcomed in the subfield we're writing for?

Hope to talk soon!

★★★

Dear reader,

A few notes to end the chapter. Our process of writing this chapter was sparked by an initial question: how can we think about the relationship between Barad's work and affect? This question does not have a straight-forward answer. Although Barad's work has been embraced within MOS generally, the affective dimensions of their framework remain underarticulated (Ringrose, Warfield and Zarabadi, 2020) and therefore also challenging to tease out and apply in our field. To unpack the affective dimensions of Barad's work, we decided to organize our writing in a way so that we not only wrote *about* affect, but *in* and *through* affect. Through this affective writing process, we became able to relate Barad's framework to issues of shame, performance, frustration, joy, care and collectivity. Or, in Barad's terminology, we became response-able★ within the complex entanglements★ we inhabit. In the writing of this chapter, we have thus become-with Barad's thinking, as we collapsed the separation between our affective community and a distanced overview of a 'theory' or 'theorist'. This is at the core of Barad's idea of intra-activity★ as the process by which things come to matter, namely as relational. This relationality was also an affective becoming, as our conversation foregrounded the collective experience of otherwise often individualized emotions, feelings or atmospheres, particularly as these played out in the organization of academic writing in the context of the COVID-19 pandemic. Importantly, this work is never finished. It continues to be open to change, to becoming anew. Through this writing we hope to invite you into the conversation, to be affected by it and produce new affect in turn.

While Barad's work on intra-action★ has become an important framework within MOS in recent years, we encourage future work to reflect on how we as researchers, and the way we organize research, come to matter in relation, and are thus affected by this work. One route we see is through the engagement with ethics★ as a relational practice of being/becoming response-able★ to the world around us. In this chapter, we provide an example of one way to approach this: Our collective writing in this chapter has aimed to collapse the binaries between the theoretical and the personal, the individual and the collective, and the human and the non-human by reading Barads works through our experiences. It hereby aims to destabilize conventional academic knowledge practices and the boundaries that define these, and instead offers the potential for different affective intra-actions to emerge. This is a political move that aims to open up space for thinking differently about the ethical premises that underpin common academic practices. We take our cue here from Thiele (2014, p. 213), who draws on Barad's idea of the always/already entangled★ nature of our being when she writes: "The different ethicality envisioned here then no longer aspires to an (always failing) responsibility for the other, with the subsequent question of which responsibility to choose in order not to either appropriate otherness into sameness or patronize others via protectionism. It instead suggests response-ability with others that transforms the ethical problem itself". We thus hope to contribute to academic practices based on collectivity, care and joy.

Hugs!

Recommended reading

Original text by Karen Barad

Barad, K. (2007). *Meeting the universe halfway. Quantum physics and the entanglement of matter and meaning*. London: Duke University Press.

Key academic text

van Amsterdam, N., van Eck, D. and Meldgaard Kjær, K. (2022). On (not) fitting in: Fat embodiment, affect and organizational materials as differentiating agents. *Organization Studies*. doi:10.1177/01708406221074162.

Accessible resource

Juelskjær, M. and Schwennesen, N. (2012). Intra-active entanglements – An interview with Karen Barad. *Kvinder, Køn & Forskning*, pp. 1–2.

References

Ashcraft, K.L. (2020). Communication as constitutive transmission? An encounter with affect. *Communication Theory*, 31(4), pp. 571, 592.

Barad, K. (1999). Agential realism. Feminist interventions in understanding scientific practices. In: M. Biagioli, ed., *The science studies reader*. London: Routledge, pp. 1–11.

Barad, K. (2003). Posthumanist performativity: Toward an understanding of how matter comes to matter. *Signs: Journal of Women in Culture and Society*, 28(3), pp. 801–831.

Barad, K. (2007). *Meeting the universe halfway: Quantum physics and the entanglement of matter and meaning*. London: Duke University Press.

Barad, K. (2008). Queer causation and the ethics of mattering. In: N. Gifney and M.J. Hird, eds., *Queering the non/human*. Aldershot: Ashgate Publishing Ltd, pp. 311–338.

Barad, K. (2010). Quantum entanglements and hauntological relations of inheritance. Dis/continuities, spacetime enfoldings, and justice-to-come. *Derrida Today*, 3(2), pp. 240–268.

Barad, K. (2012). On touching – The inhuman that therefore I am. *Differences*, 23(3), pp. 206–223.

Barad, K. (2014). Diffracting diffraction: Cutting together-apart. *Parallax*, 20(3), pp. 168–187.

Bell, E. and Vachhani, S.J. (2020). Relational encounters and vital materiality in the practice of craft work. *Organization Studies*, 41(5), pp. 681–701.

Bend, G.L. and Priola, V. (2021). 'There is nothing wrong with me': The materialisation of disability in sheltered employment. *Work, Employment and Society*. Online first. doi:10.1177/09500170211034762.

Breeze, M. (2018). Imposter syndrome as a public feeling. In: *Feeling academic in the neoliberal university*. Cham: Palgrave Macmillan, pp. 191–219.

Dale, K. and Latham, Y. (2015). Ethics and entangled embodiment: Bodies – materialities – organization. *Organization*, 22(2), pp. 166–182. doi:10.1177/1350508414 558721.

Davies, B. and Gannon, S. (2012). Collective biography and the entangled enlivening of being. *International Review of Qualitative Inquiry*, 5(4), pp. 357–376.

Ford, J., Harding, N., Gilmore, S., et al. (2017). Becoming the leader: Leadership as material presence. *Organization Studies*, 38(11), pp. 1553–1571. doi:10.1177/0170840616677633.

Gherardi, S. (2017). One turn . . . and now another one: Do the turn to practice and the turn to affect have something in common? *Management Learning*, 48(3), pp. 345–358.

Gherardi, S. (2019). Theorizing affective ethnography for organization studies. *Organization*, 26(6), pp. 741–760.

Gherardi, S., Murgia, A., Bellè, E., Miele, F. and Carreri, A. (2018). Tracking the sociomaterial traces of affect at the crossroads of affect and practice theories. *Qualitative Research in Organizations and Management: An International Journal*. https://doi.org/10.1108/QROM-04-2018-1624.

Harding, N. H., Ford, J., & Lee, H. (2017). Towards a performative theory of resistance: Senior managers and revolting subject (ivitie) s. *Organization Studies*, 38(9), 1209–1232.

Harding, N., Gilmore, S., & Ford, J. (2022). Matter that embodies: Agentive flesh and working bodies/selves. *Organization studies*, 43(5), 649–668.

Harris, K.L., McFarlane, M. and Wieskamp, V. (2020). The promise and peril of agency as motion: A feminist new materialist approach to sexual violence and sexual harassment. *Organization*, 27(5), pp. 660–679.

Huopalainen, A. (2020). Writing with the bitches. *Organization*. Online first. doi:10.1177/1350508420961533.

Jones, D.R., Visser, M., Stokes, P., Örtenblad, A., Deem, R., Rodgers, P. and Tarba, S.Y. (2020). The performative university: 'Targets', 'terror' and 'taking back freedom' in academia. *Management Learning*, 51(4), pp. 363–377.

Juelskjær, M. and Schwennesen, N. (2012). Intra-active entanglements – An interview with Karen Barad. *Kvinder, Køn & Forskning*, pp. 1–2.

Kjær, K.M. and van Amsterdam, N. (2020). Pieced together. Writing invisible (dis)abilities in academia. In: A.F. Hermann, ed., *The Routledge international handbook of organizational autoethnography*. London: Routledge, pp. 298–312.

Mandalaki, E. and Pérezts, M. (2021). Abjection overruled! Time to dismantle sexist cyberbullying in academia. *Organization*. Online first. doi:10.1177/13505084211 041711.

Moore, A. (2018). "Blackboxing it": A Poetic Min/d/ing the gap of an imposter experience in academia. *Art/Research International: A Transdisciplinary Journal*, 3(1), pp. 30–52.

Nyberg, D. (2009). Computers, customer service operatives and cyborgs: Intra-actions in call centres. *Organization Studies*, 30(11), pp. 1181–1199.

Orlikowski, W.J. (2007). Sociomaterial practices: Exploring technology at work. *Organization Studies*, 28(9), pp. 1435–1448.

Orlikowski, W.J. and Scott, S.V. (2015a). Exploring material-discursive practices. *Journal of Management Studies*, 52(5), pp. 697–705. doi:10.1111/joms.12114.

Orlikowski, W.J. and Scott, S.V. (2015b). The algorithm and the crowd: Considering the materiality of service innovation. *MIS Quarterly*, 39(1), pp. 201–216.

Ringrose, J., Warfield, K. and Zarabadi, S., eds. (2020). *Feminist posthumanisms, new materialisms and education*. London: Routledge.

Staunæs, D. and Brøgger, K. (2020). In the mood of data and measurements: Experiments as affirmative critique, or how to curate academic value with care. *Feminist Theory*, 21(4), pp. 429–445.

Symon, G. and Pritchard, K. (2015). Performing the responsive and committed employee through the sociomaterial mangle of connection. *Organization Studies*, 36(2), pp. 241–263. doi:10.1177/0170840614556914.

Thiele, K. (2014). Ethos of diffraction: New paradigms for a (post)humanist ethics. *Parallax*, 20(3), pp. 202–216. doi:10.1080/13534645.2014.927627.

van Amsterdam, N., Meldgaard-Kjær, K.M. and van Eck, D. (2022). On (not) fitting in: Fat embodiment, affect and organizational materials as differentiating agents. *Organization Studies*. Online first. doi:10.1177/01708406221074162.

van Eck, D., van Amsterdam, N. and van den Brink, M. (2021). Unsanitized writing practices: Attending to affect and embodiment throughout the research process. *Gender, Work & Organization*. Online first. doi:10.1111/gwao.12651.

Valtonen, A. and Pullen, A. (2020). Writing with rocks. *Gender, Work and Organization*. Online first. doi:10.1111/gwao.12579.

Visser, L. M., & Davies, O. E. (2021). The becoming of online healthcare through entangled power and performativity: A posthumanist agential realist perspective. *Organization Studies*, 42(12), 1817–1837.

7 Corporeal Ethics in the More-Than-Human World (Rosalyn Diprose)

Veera Kinnunen

Introduction

An almost impenetrable stench is lingering in our backyard. Things like excrement to vomit come to mind. It sure does s-t-i-n-k! The smell reminds me of pig manure on my great aunt's farm. I go to the nearby forest, start digging holes in the ground and bury the matter there. I fill the holes with dirt and decaying leaves, hoping that the cover is enough to seal the smell in. Having done it, I do not feel particularly elated. I have to ask myself whether inhaling such air – welcoming this stinking cloud of microbial life into my body – is even healthy. Might it even be dangerous? Once again, I am ready to give up, to quit trying.

The incident described earlier is a quote from my autoethnographic field diary about my bokashi composting experiments that I have been conducting since 2016. In the excerpt, I describe one of my most disruptive experiences with bokashi composting. In the course of the past five years, I have developed a well-functioning bokashi routine, but I still regularly face difficulties like the incident described earlier. I keep falling in and out of love with my bokashi bucket. So far, we have had some lengthy break-ups, but we have always resumed our relationship. Fortunately, the unsettling events are outnumbered by countless satisfying moments in which I have witnessed the transformation of waste matter into rich, sour smelling soil.

Although I cannot say that I have enjoyed those experiences, they are in many ways at the core of my research. My experiments with bokashi have given flesh to feminist philosopher Rosalyn Diprose's words: "The other affects me, gets under my skin, and that is why I am made to think" (Diprose, 2002, p. 126). The disgusting smell has affective power to make me retch and, hence, it forces me to act. The smell even makes me think, as breathing in the smelly air makes me painfully aware of the possibly dangerous microbial presence and the porousness of my bodily tissues. Living with bokashi has taught me a great deal about the ethical

DOI: 10.4324/9781003182887-7

importance of remaining open to difference – whilst respecting the difference of the other.

In my early musings about bokashi composting, I was interested in ethics of waste and I was inspired by Diprose's thoughts on embodied ethics. In her book *Corporeal Generosity* (2002), Diprose develops radical generosity by stressing the role of sentient bodies relating to other bodies as a prerequisite for thinking and acting differently. Thinking with my bokashi compost and following in the footsteps of cultural theorist Hawkins (2005), it made sense to propose that unsettling, affective encounters with matter are ethical moments from which new habits and relations can emerge.

Since those early days, I have continued to experiment and think with my bokashi compost, and my thinking has been nourished with a range of more-than-human theorists, such as Haraway, Barad, Hamilton, Neimanis, Shotwell, Tsing, Swanson, and Mol, to name but a few. As it often happens, the works of some foundational thinkers become so thoroughly incorporated in the theory, that they become, if not completely erased, at least diluted and unidentified. As a result, the names of those thinkers disappear from literature reviews and reference lists. Browsing through my recent texts, it seems that this has indeed happened to Diprose. The underlying idea of corporeal generosity has been mulched into my own thinking up to the point that, at present, it is almost impossible to tease out Diprose's influence. This should not come as a surprise. First of all, as the number of theorists and publications keeps growing exponentially, naming every piece of writing that one has been influenced by during one's academic career would be an impossible task and would result in incomprehensible and unengaging texts. Second, it has been noted that female authors[1] experience this dilution more frequently than their male colleagues.

Although Diprose's early phenomenological work on corporeal generosity may have influenced the work of some major contemporary thinkers within more-than-human theorizing addressing the issue of ethics, a quick browse through the reference lists of seminal texts by thinkers such as Alaimo (2010), Bennett (2010), Zylinska (2014), Shotwell (2016), Haraway (2014), Latimer and Puig de la Bellacasa (2013), Puig de la Bellacasa (2017, 2019), Fournier (2020) reveals that reference to Diprose has been omitted from these contributions.[2]

Haraway, among others, has called for a feminist citational practice which would be "precise about the history of ideas and the particular creativity and originality and importance of other women's thinking" (Haraway in Terranova documentary, quoted in Hamilton and Neimanis, 2018, p. 517). Hamilton and Neimanis (2018, p. 503) have proposed *composting* as a feminist metaphor and strategy for acknowledging concepts and commitments that have been foundational to the emergence of a scholarly approach. Taking a lead from Hamilton and Neimanis, I understand composting as a feminist exercise to make politics of citation. Rather than aiming for a genealogical review tracing the development of embodied ethics as a concept, composting has a more modest aim of acknowledging how phenomenological, corporeal generosity has fed my current more-than-human approach. Moreover, I seek to trace the lineage from Diprose's embodied phenomenological ethics to feminist organizational ethics, and more-than-human formulations on ethics in organizations.

In preparation for this chapter, I have delved into my intellectual compost pile and returned to Diprose's writings in an attempt to acknowledge how more-than-human theorization has been (and could further be) nourished with the feminist concept of corporeal ethics. I begin with a close reading of Diprose's *Corporeal Generosity* and her conceptualization of embodied ethics. I continue to map how the notion has sparked ethical imagination in the field of feminist organization studies. I then bring the notion into dialogue with more recent writings on more-than-human ethics. By doing so, I hope to illustrate that feminist theorization on corporeal generosity has not only sparked anthropocentric feminist ethics in organization studies but also had implications for feminist naturecultural thought, although these two threads of feminist theorization have developed largely as parallel strands. I conclude by returning to my bokashi bucket.

Inspired by the feminist idea of inseparability of theory and praxis, I follow Diprose's urge to *write with blood* – or perhaps even more descriptive of my work – with *soil stained fingers*, as Hamilton and Neimanis (2018, p. 524) have put it. In this text, to write with blood means that I will illustrate the fleshiness of corporeal ethics through my personal, embodied encounters with decaying and transforming waste matter.

Embodying ethics

Ethics as a historical field of thought can be roughly understood as a 'system intended to guide individuals in their decision-making' (Sherwin, 2008, p. 11), that is, to enable assessing rights and wrongs in a quest to obtain a 'good life' or 'happiness', whatever those may be. In short, ethics is about being positioned and taking a position in relation to others (Diprose, 2002, p. 238). Feminist thinkers, Diprose among them, have criticized canonical Western theories of ethics for placing an individual capable of moral judgement at the centre of ethical thought. Western social imaginaries have been dominated by the masculine idea of rational contract and exchange between autonomous individuals, at the expense of relational, embodied and affective aspects of sociality (Diprose, 2002, p. 171). Although historical theories of ethics have assessed moral formation in the context of collectives, they nevertheless typically (if not always) assume an individual moral actor, a person who 'knows, wills and acts' (Shotwell, 2016, p. 108). Canonical articulations from Aristotle's virtue ethics to Mill's utilitarianism centre around this individual moral agent. Whereas Aristotle suggested that ethics was based on individual virtues of 'man', Kant defined the moral agent as capable of making rational decisions in accordance with the universal 'moral laws'. Even Mill's utilitarian theory aiming for the greatest possible good was intended to enable the individual to ensure that he does not violate rights of the others while seeking his own benefit (Shotwell, 2016, pp. 108–109). In an attempt to defy the universalizing ethical canon, feminist scholars have situated *bodies* at the centre of their ethical theorizing (Bergoffen and Weiss, 2011, p. 453).

In *Corporeal Generosity. On giving with Nietzsche, Merleau-Ponty, and Levinas* (Diprose, 2002), Diprose develops a social imaginary of *radical generosity* as an alternative to logics of rational exchange between individuals. Diprose builds her revised formulation of ethics on phenomenological ontology, which gives primacy to the body and intersubjectivity. I will next elaborate the mode of ethics that follows from these two assumptions.

First, Diprose builds from *embodiment* as a fundamental grounding of human existence and a prerequisite for community formation. This move implies downplaying rational calculation as a central feature of ethics, and emphasising the pre-reflective, affective aspects of knowing and being. Following Merleau-Ponty, Diprose contents that it is the *affective enjoyment* experienced when thinking, reading, sleeping and warming oneself in the sun, which nourishes all human activity, and explains "why we bother at all". Embodied ways of being become routinized into corporeal habits – "cultural-historical sediments" – that provide a familiar, unquestioned atmosphere which, in turn, informs my ways of being and relating with others. Personal perceptions as well as moral judgements and decisions are filtered through the sediments of lived experiences and encounters, which is why "I will tend to perceive and respond to my world in a similar way to how I have before" (Diprose, 2013, p. 196). This subtle sedimentation of "corporeal styles" results in a tendency to treat the objects of the world as fixed facts, which closes off possibilities for other ways of existing for oneself and with the others (Diprose, 2002, p. 120).

Second, Diprose begins her theorising from the fundamental intersubjectivity of human bodies. Rather than embracing the notion of individual autonomy as an ethical ideal, she insists that community formation rests on *intercorporeality*. That is, my sensing, perceiving body is never just "mine", but always constituted in relation to other bodies, and informed by social imaginaries that come before my own (Diprose, 2002, pp. 193–194). Therefore, cultural-historical sedimentations that govern "my" perception are always accumulated in intersubjective experiences (Diprose, 2002, p. 39). Actions or thoughts that affectively feel familiar and "right" are a result of cultural-historical sedimentation accumulated in intersubjective experiences, through embodied gestures that non-verbally affirm or judge, such as a warm smile, an appreciative tap in the back or a frown (Diprose, 2002, pp. 38–39). Judgements are made first through intercorporeal, sedimented cultural-historical social imaginaries that "make sense", and rationalization is added afterwards. Even institutional values, cemented in laws, policies and principles, are filtered through these sediments, as the makers and guardians of laws and policies are informed by the intercorporeally transmitted social imaginaries that is "in them" through perception, which is "pre-reflective, affective, and thoroughly corporeal" (Diprose, 2002, pp. 174–175).

If our perceptions are filtered through intercorporeal sedimentations, which shape our modes of being together, the question remains: What possibilities for change exist? Diprose reminds us that despite our tendency to treat the objects that we perceive in our everyday lives as unquestioned and finished, their character is constantly open and contested. Perceptions, values and meanings are being actualized by and through the bodies every time they are being expressed. Therefore, change is always possible as soon as this unfinished and reciprocally produced character of things becomes exposed. In order to expose the unfinished nature of things and set us on the path of thinking differently, the convenience of the domain of familiarity characterized by sedimented habits needs to be somehow shaken.

To theorize the possibility for change, Diprose turns to Levinasian ethics of generosity. Ethics arises when one lets oneself to be affected by the alterity of others, which opens up a possibility for being otherwise (Diprose, 2002, p. 14). Drawing from Levinas, Diprose suggests that *being open to difference* is the ethical principle forming the basis of community formation (Diprose, 2002, p. 136). Being faced with the alterity, the feeling that he or she cannot be known, arouses affective response, "touches me, affects me, cuts me, and opens me to the other and to the world". Therefore, unsettling *encounters*, in which the alterity of the other is experienced and welcomed, are at the heart of ethics, where new paths for thinking and living may arise (Diprose, 2002, p. 132; 2013; Levinas, 1987, p. 47, *Philosophy and the idea of infinity*.)

Complementing Levinasian thought with phenomenological embodiment, Diprose emphasizes that ethical encounters are thoroughly corporeal and affective – the taken-for-grantedness of being-in-the world is shaken through being open to the alterity of the other, by affecting and being affected by other bodies (Diprose, 2002, p. 71). Unsettling embodied encounters with the otherness of the other disturb and shake the familiar ways of being: "the other affects me, gets under my skin, and that is why I am made to think" (Diprose, 2002, p. 126).

According to Diprose, there is a moral dimension in encountering otherness: "the disturbing experience of the other's alterity urges me not to turn my back" (Diprose, 2002, p. 137). Ethical responsibility derives from encountering the alterity of the other, which demands, literally, a *response*: The other's teaching of alterity solicits a response, which forms the basis of my ability to respond at all to anything (Diprose, 2002, p. 137). The other's otherness is what makes me feel, and furthermore, makes me think what I feel and thus creates responsibility through demanding a response (Diprose, 2002, p. 137).

Politics of generosity as a mode of staying open to difference is at the heart of feminist project of reconfiguring ethics in organizations. Feminist organization scholars have emphasized the need to acknowledge the ethical and political potential of pre-reflective, affective resonances and emotional commitments like care and compassion (see, e.g. Kenny and Fotaki, 2015; Pors, 2019). I will next elaborate how scholars in feminist organization studies have embraced and developed corporeal ethics as a radical alternative to conventional business ethics.

From corporate to corporeal ethics

The notion of corporeal generosity has been especially influential in feminist organization and management studies where attempts have been made to formulate radical alternatives to the conventional business ethics. By emphasizing the situated and embodied character of ethics, feminist organizational ethics have sought to overcome the divide between ethics embedded in the micro practices of everyday organizational life and the macro-institutional ethical codes of conduct (Pullen and Rhodes, 2014; see also Hancock, 2008; Küpers, 2015, for further critique on conventional business ethics and development of embodied ethics in organizations). Drawing from feminist ethics, scholars have criticized corporate business ethics for being based on utilitarian, calculative reasoning, locating ethics in the organizational practice and codes of conduct (Küpers,

2015, p. 30; Pullen and Rhodes, 2014). For instance, Pullen and Rhodes (2014) have argued that organizational ethics has – thus far – failed to recognize the affective side of inter-personal ethical engagements as well as the significance of situated encounters. Even on the rare occasions when the ethical significance of human interaction has been acknowledged, it has still been conceived as "disembodied, rational, decision based and/or cognitively deliberate" (Pullen and Rhodes, 2014, p. 6).

Drawing from Diprose's work, Pullen and Rhodes (2013, 2014) propose an ethics grounded in 'embodied, lived experience' as an alternative to approaches concentrating on the ethical agency of the organization as an entity. They develop a mode of embodied organizational ethics that precedes and exceeds rational schemes seeking to provide general sets of conditions that promote ethical behaviour among members of an organization. Embodied organizational ethics is not a strict code of conduct, but, rather, originates from "emergent and affective experience" with other bodies (Pullen and Rhodes, 2014, p. 159). Their understanding of ethics is in line with that of Diprose, for whom ethics is openness towards the difference of the other, a form of generosity in which the 'other' is given priority over 'self' as one is called to assume responsibility for the other, in the sense of demanding a response instead of turning one's back to the other when encountering alterity.

The feminist organizational ethics seeks to disrupt the hierarchical normativity of society, the norms and social imaginaries of which support 'bodies that already dominate', and exclude others, namely, 'women, indigenous peoples, working-class men and others' (Diprose, 2002, p. 171). Therefore, for feminist organizational ethics, living, feeling and sensate bodies are the primary sites for resistance, from which alterity and difference can be recognized and embraced. Turning attention to the ethical potential of affective encounters offers an ethicopolitical space for resistance in organizations. As Pullen and Rhodes put it, embodied ethics is an explicitly political project in that it seeks to "dispel the forms of violent categorization and hierarchization that privilege those few who are able to conform to the power of the which is institutionalized as normal" (Pullen and Rhodes, 2014, p. 164). Corporeal ethics urges one to sensitize oneself to the alterity of the other in order to work against the social imaginaries that establish "privileged ways of being, including one's own, thereby reducing sexed or cultural identity, to isolate, corporeal units, singled out for exchange, usury, judgement, correction, condemnation or ridicule" (Diprose, 2002, p. 194).

The examples I have offered so far have been anthropocentric in their scope. In seeking to disrupt the dominant, masculine normativity enacted in organizations, feminist organization studies have mainly focused on welcoming *other people's difference* (Pullen and Rhodes, 2014, p. 160; for exception, see Dale and Latham 2015). The responsibility towards alterity of the other has been understood to be formed when encountering other humans. However, despite being an important site of resistance, power relations are not enacted only within embodied encounters between humans. Human bodies are fundamentally inter-related with other bodies that are all too easily separated into taken-for-granted others, such as 'resources', 'livestock', 'technology', or 'nature'. How, then, might it be possible to be open to ethical claims of other-than-human bodies? How to pursue an ethics that would recognise human responsibility but would not take human scale and human interest as its core (Kinnunen and Valtonen, 2017, pp. 5–6). Corporeal ethics may offer valuable lessons for decentering humans from ethical thought (Rantala, Valtonen and Salmela, 2020).

I propose that political potential of corporeal generosity does not have to be limited to intercorporeal resonances between *human bodies*. Following Diprose, corporeal ethics "defies the culturally informed habits of perception and judgement that would perpetuate injustice by shoring up body integrity, singular identity, and their distinction between inside and outside, culture and nature, self and other" (Diprose, 2002, p. 190). Therefore, corporeal generosity may offer means to bridge the splits not only between body and mind but also between nature and culture, which have been so eagerly embraced and perpetuated in the Western intellectual tradition.

In the next section, I will elaborate on how ethical responsibilities made through acknowledging our inextricable embodiment and intercorporeality have been approached in emerging posthuman feminist thought.

Posthuman feminist ethics

The array of anthropogenic environmental threats that the world is facing at present and in the near future – among them climate change, biodiversity loss, air and water pollution and shortage of water – is nothing short of daunting. This situation demands critical self-reflection of traditionally human-centric research traditions. The current environmental emergency, often referred to as a new geological epoch of the *Anthropocene*,[3] has urged humanities and social sciences to reconsider the often Eurocentric and rationalistic assumptions underlying in ethical theories and to seek an ethics that takes not only people and – at best, animals – but all kinds of non-human entities and materialities into account. It has become clear that it is problematic to separate 'the human' from 'the natural' and refer to the former as 'the cultural', even for analytic purposes. Materially and relationally oriented feminist scholarship has made pioneering work in pinpointing the problematic 'ontological splits' (Haraway, 1991) inscribed in the Western intellectual tradition. They have pointed out that human exceptionalism is one of its most striking biases, which has resulted in failure to recognise the entanglement of humans and the rest of the world (Puig de la Bellacasa, 2017; Zylinska, 2014). Thus, feminist posthuman ethics begins, first, from identifying the inextricable entanglement of natural and cultural phenomena, and second, from acknowledging that practices of knowing and being are not separated from ethics (see, e.g. Barad, 2007; Haraway, 2008; Puig de la Bellacasa, 2017).

Feminist posthuman scholarship has made ground-breaking work with developing ethics in these 'compromised times' (Shotwell, 2016). For instance, Puig de la Bellacasa and Shotwell, among others, have taken the idea of intercorporeality even further and emphasized the multispecies interdependency as a condition of being. Along this line of thought, interdependency entails being "embedded in all forms of life – humans and their technologies, animals, plants, microorganisms, elemental resources such as air and water, as well as the soil we feed on" (Puig de la Bellacasa, 2017, p. 129). Intercorporeality creates an ethical implication by stressing that human survival is intimately dependent on living, sentient, human and non-human others. Moreover, radical relationality implies that what are conceived as 'bodies' are not separate entities with clear-cut boundaries, but, more accurately, co-emergent becomings dispersed across space and time (e.g. Shotwell, 2016, p. 120). Rather than freeing humans from obligations, embodied relationality suggests that becoming aware of our foundational interdependence – being stuck inside relations of suffering – generates an obligation to respond (Shotwell, 2016, p. 127). Neither does it wipe away differences and power-relations within webs of dependence: capacities for taking action (and modes of acting) – say, of contaminated ground water – are different for a microbe, a baby or a politician. Each of those agents is stuck in different webs of relations, allowing for different responses.

Despite being at least somewhat separate strands of thought, posthuman ethics of interdependency has much in common with embodied feminist ethics. First of all, both strands share feminism's ethico-political ambit to transform worldly relations into more inclusive ones, whilst staying open to difference. Both strands also oppose the Western philosophical canon by arguing against individualized ethics which turns ethics into a rational choice of atomized selves, and suggest an alternative mode of ethics by building on embodiment and relationality. They also refuse to start theorizing ethics from a normative perspective, and do so by attuning to the particular and situated aspects of ethicality (as opposed to strict codes of conduct) and by paying attention to embodied encounters, affective disturbances and ethical cuts. However, along with their similarities, the two strands of thought also have differences in emphases. Feminist embodied ethics in organizations has mainly focused on inequality between human bodies and has approached *affective embodiment* as a site of resistance from which to attend to difference and fight against masculine normativity and oppression, whereas posthuman theorizing has shifted away from anthropocentrism by theorising *relations* (within which bodies emerge) as the smallest unit of analysis and by attuning to the co-emergence of *multispecies worlds*.

I am interested in probing the possibility of combining these ethical commitments in order to be able to approach both human and non-human struggles simultaneously – to attend to inequalities and injustices without putting the human at the centre stage. In the remainder of the chapter, I return to Diprose's formulation on *corporeal generosity* in an attempt to merge afore described two veins of ethical thought into practice. Through my affective engagement with my bokashi bucket, I seek to open myself to the alterity of the non-human others, such as the microbial presence of decaying organic matter, and listen to their teachings. I call this exercise *corporeal generosity beyond human exceptionalism.*

Compost ethics

I am still hovering over my compost container. Every cell in my body is screaming a warning: "Back off. Something has gone seriously wrong". I resist the affective urge to withdraw from the container, and carefully inhale the smelly air in an attempt to figure out the chemical composition of its lively contents. I wonder if it could be butyric acid, since I have heard that its smell resembles pig manure. What happens when I inhale this thick stench into my lungs? How will it affect my body? How can I tell whether it is dangerous to me? Should I wear rubber gloves? And what do the neighbours think?

For Diprose, disturbing moments like this are moments in which something goes under my skin, and makes me think differently. The strangeness of the other penetrates one's skin and thus animates the body. Moreover, Diprose emphasizes that being exposed to and affected by the world is deeply active and political, as it informs my moral judgements and actions at a pre-reflective level. Politics and ontology are thus inseparable from ethics (Diprose, 2002, p. 14). Veijola et al. formulate the world-changing potential of disruptive encounters beautifully in the context of tourism research:

> When we are confronted with the unexpected, the unfamiliar or the illegible, we can no longer affirm our old ways of thinking, feeling and acting, but have to find alternative, perhaps radical, ways of connecting with others, ourselves, and the environment. Different affects are at play in these moments of disruption, affects such as fear, loathing and aversion may be replaced with more ethical ways of relating with the unknown others.
>
> (Veijola et al., 2014, p. 3)

Inhaling the stinky air from my compost gone awry made me painfully aware of the fleshy liveliness of the waste matter and the porosity of my own body. The thick smell in the air made me realize that just by standing next to the compost, my bodily tissues became imbued with the microbial liveliness of the unruly substance. In this situation, the possibly hazardous multitude of microbial life went under my skin through my respiratory system, through the skin of my bare hands, reminding me that my body was not separate from my compost in any real sense. By the same token, it became clear to me that the microbes – in all their alterity – were not just occasional visitors that had penetrated my body through my skin: They had been *under my skin* all along. In fact, I was, or at least what I used to consider my *self* – was materially co-constituted by a multitude of those unknown others. At that very moment, the realization was not intellectual, but rather, I sensed the porosity of 'me' affectively in my tissues. It took a while until I was able to formulate this sensuous realization into intelligible words.

Nevertheless, this affective event stayed with me and made me think. I kept coming back to that moment weeks and months after the incident that effectively shook me from the security of my existing patterns of being, and brought me to a heightened awareness of there being other modes of being and living in the world. To me, this encounter came to exemplify more-than-human corporeal ethics in praxis. Indeed, looking back, it seems like a world-changing moment. From then on, I was not the same, neither was my compost. A new ethical configuration had emerged: from then on, we were in this world together.

In my previous work, I have been re-thinking waste relations with my bokashi by celebrating microbial togetherness of the world and more-than-human ecologies that bokashi making enacts (Kinnunen, 2021). In line with the principles of feminist embodied ethics, I have represented bokashi making as an everyday act of resistance, working against formal and inflexible regulations of institutional waste management. Indeed, bokashi making disrupts common imaginaries of waste as an external threat, and, by requiring attuning to the liveliness of the microbial world and even collaboration with it, promotes imaginaries of symbiotic interdependence. Following Hawkins (2005), I have proposed that a new ethics of waste could be based on recognizing the interdependency and multiplicity of the more-than-human world, on taking responsibility even for things and materialities that one leaves behind and tries to forget (Hawkins, 2005, p. 115).

This time, I try to push my thinking a little further. The exercise in combining feminist more-than-human and embodied ethics (see also Fournier, 2020) urges me to stay with the contradictions present in this encounter by asking: Who or what are left out of these relations? Whose work/suffering makes this relation possible? What kinds of 'others' are present, and how to stay open to difference?

First of all, although we bokashi practitioners often contrast our bokashi making with normative, industrially organized institutional waste management, my bokashi making is not as separate from institutional waste infrastructure as I would like to think, but rather thoroughly conditioned by it: By taking care of recycling of non-organic surplus, such as plastics, cardboards, and metals, our modern, well-functioning waste infrastructure allows me to concentrate on bokashi making. Second, making bokashi is not an unconditional welcoming of all beings, be they waste materials, bacteria or other living creatures. I do not allow, for instance, plastics, 'toxins' or pathogenic combinations like butyric acid or sciarid flies enter my bokashi bucket. Although I fearlessly engage with unruly microbial combinations that the bokashi process produces, I have developed a set of practices to keep the 'bokashi soil' free of pesticides and other toxins, a luxury not available to everyone as pointed out by, e.g. Davies (2018) and Shotwell (2016).

I have heard comments that worrying about what my neighbours might think is a human-centred act, which might be interpreted as a sign of superficial morality: privileging the appearances over caring for the wellbeing of bokashi. However, living in a rowhouse in a densely populated suburb, I have obligations to my neighbours. The dense stenches are not only teasing my sensory registers, but theirs, too. Through the smells, the decaying matter – which I was responsible for, because it had been generated as a result of my actions – had demanded a response from me. My response was not to turn my back on it by throwing it in the trash, for instance, but to take responsibility by mixing it with the microbiota of healthy soil in the nearby woods.

However, when I buried the matter in the forest, new ethical cuts were revealed: Whether I committed a crime is a question of boundaries, depending on whether the matter was defined as 'soil' or as 'waste'. According to the Finnish Waste Act, I have different obligations regarding waste than regarding soil. Moreover, when I made the hasty decision to bury the matter in the ground, I thought about the well-being of my bokashi, my family and my neighbours. I never stopped thinking about my obligations to the earth where I buried the bokashi matter. As I had been told that "the soil doesn't mind the smell", I didn't stop for a moment to consider the new interrelations that I possibly created by introducing a batch of fertile humus to the podzol land with low nutrients. Despite my motivating will to care for the earth, I forgot to be mindful of difference: there is no such thing as a general 'earth' or 'soil'. The fertile soil in my small garden plot is a whole different ecology of relations compared to the soil in the mixed woodland. They need different kind of response, and I have different obligations to them.

This example reveals that I am easily drawn to expressing moral superiority for taking care of the Earth by composting my organic waste, without considering carefully that ethics is not about individual consumption choices. If ethics was about the righteous individual choices and moral deeds (such as sorting wastes, paying CO_2 compensations or buying fair trade food) then it would be diminished into something that the rich have the ability to possess (Shotwell, 2016, p. 125). I have to admit that making bokashi does not turn me and my bokashi morally superior beings, but rather, I can afford to delve into loving and playful experiments with my unruly microbial companions and waste materials, because I possess a privileged position providing me a spacious home and plenty of spare time. Even in an affluent Western context I have the rare luxury of turning my hobbies into work by researching them.

More-than-human generosity

Making bokashi has become my daily exercise of practicing more-than-human ethics of generosity.

Practicing bokashi has transformed my environment through enriching its microbial abundance, but affective engagement with bokashi matter has also transformed me more profoundly through altering my imagination. *I* have became *we*. Yet, I have also learned to admit that I will never be able to fully know or control my bokashi. It will always remain a constantly transforming, living entity with a life beyond my control.

Living with a bokashi compost teaches a feel for the diversity of being-in-the-world through encounters with the other – including those that are already within me – and tolerance for the possibility of contamination. Bokashi composting has provided me with countless everyday instances of staying open to the troubling presence of the unknown others – sometimes with affective force of repulsion and loathing, but often with curiosity and awe.

Coming back to the unsettling encounter with my bokashi, and staying open to its teachings, made me realise that there was even more for me to learn than just celebration of mutual relations with waste matter and microbial cultures. While I became aware of the presence of microbes within and around me, there were other beings that were closed out of these relations so efficiently that they escaped my perception. I also failed to stay open to difference between different materialities and different obligations. Practicing bokashi composting thus teaches me to recognise my complicated – and not always beneficial – relations with abjected others, such as waste, microbes, soils and insects, but also to be mindful of my own positioning with other humans.

Thinking with Diprose (2002, p. 188) "politics of generosity begins with all of us, it begins and remains in trouble, and it begins with the act". It is about willingness to be open to the alterity of the other and to respond to it; it is about writing – whether with blood or with soil-stained fingers – stories of living together in this world.

Notes

1   And, one might add, indigenous and POC thinkers (see Liboiron, 2021).
2   Jennifer Hamilton and Astrida Neimanis (2018, p. 519) pay attention to this absence by commenting that the discussion on material intercorporeality in the environmental humanities would benefit from closer reading of feminist embodied phenomenology such as Rosalyn Diprose as well as Luce Irigaray, Helene Cixous, Gail Weiss and Margrit Schildrick, whose ideas are incorporated in "more contemporary expressions of connected embodiment" such as Stacy Alaimo's transcorporeality and Astrida Neimanis's bodies of water.
3   Anthropocene, "The epoch of Man", is defined by the impact of humans on geological, biological and climatic planetary processes (Crutzen and Stoermer, 2000). On ethics in the age of the Anthropocene, see e.g. Zylinska (2014) and Rantala and Farah (2020).

Recommended reading

Original text by Rosalyn Diprose

Diprose, R. (2003). *Corporeal generosity: On giving with Nietzsche, Merleau-Ponty, and Levinas.* Albany: SUNY-Press.

Key academic text

Pullen, A. and Rhodes, C. (2022). *Organizing corporeal ethics. A research overview*. London and New York: Routledge.

Accessible text

Kinnunen, V. and Valtonen, A. (2017). *Living ethics in a more-than-human world*. Rovaniemi: University of Lapland. https://urn.fi/URN:ISBN:978-952-337-046-3.

References

Alaimo, S. (2010). *Bodily natures: Science, environment, and the material self*. Bloomington: Indiana University Press.

Barad, K. (2007). *Meeting the universe halfway. Quantum physics and the entanglement of matter and meaning*. Durham: Duke University Press.

Bennett, J. (2010). *Vibrant matter. A political ecology of things*. Durham and London: Duke University Press.

Bergoffen, D. and Weiss, G. (2011). Embodying the ethical. Editor's introduction. *Hypatia*, 26(3), pp. 453–460.

Crutzen, P. J. and Stoermer, E. F. (2000). The 'Anthropocene'. *Global Change Newsletter*, 41: pp. 17–18.

Dale, K. and Latham, Y. (2015). Ethics and entangled embodiment: Bodies-materialities-organization. *Organization*, 22(2), pp. 166–182. doi:10.1177/1350508414558721.

Davies, T. (2018). Toxic space and time: Slow violence, necropolitics, and petrochemical pollution. *Annals of the American Association of Geographers*, 108(6), pp. 1537–1553.

Diprose, R. (2002). *Corporeal generosity: On giving with Nietzsche, Merleau-Ponty, and Levinas*. Albany: SUNY-Press.

Diprose, R. (2013). Corporeal interdependence: From vulnerability to dwelling in ethical community. *SubStance*, 42(3), pp. 185–204. Available at: www.jstor.org/stable/24540731.

Fournier, L. (2020). Fermenting feminism as methodology and metaphor: Approaching transnational feminist practices through microbial transformation. *Environmental Humanities*, 12(1), pp. 88–112. https://doi.org/10.1215/22011919-8142220.

Hamilton, J.M. and Neimanis, A. (2018). Composting feminisms and environmental humanities. *Environmental Humanities*, 10(2), pp. 501–526.

Hancock, P. (2008). Embodied generosity and an ethics of organization. *Organization Studies*, 29(10), pp. 1357–1373. doi:10.1177/0170840608093545.

Haraway, D. (1991). *Simians, cyborgs, and women. The reinvention of nature*. London and New York: Routledge.

Haraway, D. (2008). *When species meet*. Minneapolis and London: University of Minnesota Press.

Haraway, D. (2014). *Anthropocene, capitalocene, chtulucene*. Open Transcripts. Available at: http://opentranscripts.org/transcript/anthropocene-capitalocene-chthulucene/.

Hawkins, G. (2005). *The ethics of waste: How we relate to rubbish*. Lanham: Rowman and Littlefield Publishers.

Kenny, K. and Fotaki, M. (2015). From gendered organizations to compassionate borderspaces: Reading corporeal ethics with Bracha Ettinger. *Organization*, 22(2), pp. 183–199. doi:10.1177/1350508414558723.

Kinnunen, V. (2021). Knowing, being, and living with bokashi. In: S. Brives, M. Rest, and S. Sariola, eds., *With microbes*. Manchester: Mattering Press.

Kinnunen, V. and Valtonen, A. (2017). Towards living ethics. In: V. Kinnunen and A. Valtonen, eds., *Living ethics in a more-than-human world*. Rovaniemi: University of Lapland, pp. 5–11.

Küpers, W. (2015). Embodied responsive ethical practice. The contribution of Merleau-Ponty for a Corporeal Ethics in organisations. *Electronic Journal of Business Ethics and Organization Studies*, 20(1), pp. 30–45.

Latimer, J. and Puig de la Bellacasa, M. (2013). Rethinking the ethical: Everyday shifts of care in biogerontology. In: N. Priaulx and A. Wrigley, eds., *Ethics, Law & Society: Volume V*. London & New York: Routledge, pp. 153–174.

Levinas, E. (1987). Philosophy and the idea of infinity. In: A. Lingis, trans., *Emmanuel levinas. Collected philosophical papers*. Dordrecht: Martinus Nijhoff.

Liboiron, M. (2021). *Pollution is colonialism*. Durham and London: Duke University Press.

Pors, J.G. (2019). The political and ethical potential of affective resonance between bodies. In: M. Fotaki and A. Pullen, eds., *Diversity, affect and embodiment in organizing*. London: Palgrave Macmillan.

Puig de la Bellacasa, M. (2017). *Matters of care. Speculative ethics in more than human worlds*. Minneapolis: Minnesota Press.

Puig de La Bellacasa, M. (2019). Re-animating soils: transforming human–soil affections through science, culture and community. *The Sociological Review*, 67(2), pp. 391–407.

Pullen, A. and Rhodes, C. (2013). Corporeal ethics and the politics of resistance in organizations. *Organization*, 21(6), pp. 782–796.

Pullen, A. and Rhodes, C. (2014). Ethics, embodiment and organizations. *Organization*, 22(2), pp. 159–165.

Rantala, O., Valtonen, A. and Salmela, T. (2020). Walking with rocks – with care. In: A. Valtonen O. Rantala, and P.D. Farah, eds., *Ethics and politics of space for the Anthropocene*. Cheltenham and Northampton: Edward Elgar Publishing, pp. 35–50.

Sherwin, S. (2008). Whither bioethics? How feminisms can help reorient bioethics. *International Journal of Feminist Approaches to Bioethics*, 1, pp. 7–27.

Shotwell, A. (2016). *Against purity. Living ethically in compromised times*. Minneapolis: Minnesota Press.

Veijola, S., Molz, J.G., Pyyhtinen, O., Höckert, E. and Grit, A. (2014). *Disruptive tourism and its untidy guests. Alternative ontologies for future hospitalities*. London: Palgrave Macmillan.

Zylinska, J. (2014). *Minimal ethics for the Anthropocene*. Ann Harbour: Open Humanities Press.

Index

academia 24–25, 80–81, 86, 87–89
activism 4, 6
affect: ability to 13, 15–16, 24, 29, 64; occurrences of 1–2, 13, 22, 97; ordinary 29–30, 32–34, 36, 40; organizational 21, 24; as political 5, 17, 24
affected, as state of being 13, 15–16, 19–21
affective: connections 47–48, 53; ethics 81; relations 16, 49, 52; response 96; solidarity 4; turn 12, 20–21
affective organisation 15–16, 19, 22–23
agency 3, 48, 62, 66, 77, 733
Ahmed, Sara 3, 5–6, 8, 12–21, 23
Anthropocene 55, 99; anthropocentrism 76, 101
anti-racist 6, 23
Ashcraft, Karen Lee 24, 77
attuned 15–16, 19, 24, 30–31
attunement: atmospheric 34, 65; state of being happy 15
auto-ethnography 92

bacteria 61, 103
Barad, Karen 5, 8, 76–82, 84–86, 87–88, 93
becomings 7, 49, 84, 100
Bell, Emma 24, 81–82
Bennett, Jane 3, 5, 8, 61–72, 93
Berlant, Lauren 5, 35, 37
beyonding 48
Black Lives Matter 25
blackness 17, 22, 25
blasphemy 7, 47
bodies: human 3, 37, 77, 96, 99, 101; non-human 3, 8, 63, 67; see also more-than-human

bokashi: bucket 94, 101, 102–103; compost 92–93, 105
breathing 61, 72
brick wall 18, 20
Butler, Judith 5

Christensen, Jannick 6, 21, 23
collage 7, 40–41
community: affective 12, 14–15, 88; feminist 8, 76; formation 95–96; pride 23
conversation: affective 76; daydreaming 29; e-mail 77–78, 83
corporeal: ethics 5, 92, 97–99; generosity 93–94, 97, 99, 101
COVID-19 35, 48, 77, 80, 84, 88
culture 29, 32, 38, 40, 50, 99
cyborg 7, 50

DeLanda, Manuel 37
Deleuze, Gilles 37, 40, 63, 69
demons 50
diffraction 78–79, 81; diffractively 77, 79–80
Diprose, Rosalyn 3, 5, 8, 93–99, 101, 105
diversity 18–19, 22–23, 66
Douglas, Mary 5

embodiment: affective 95, 101; gendered 79, 81
emotion: alignment with 14–15, 20–21; flow of 18–19
enchantment 7, 61
encounters: organizational 3, 8, 98, 101; surprising 33, 37, 66, 93, 96
entanglement 2–4, 50, 80, 87, 100

environment 61, 66–67, 76, 99, 104
ethicopolitical 98
ethics: business 46, 53, 97; organizational 9, 66, 72, 97–98; *see also* feminist
ethnography 30
experience: actual 1, 40, 83; aesthetic 31–32; affective 4, 39, 98; disturbing 51–52, 97, 101; sensory 29, 34, 37, 40, 103
exposed 8, 96, 101

familiarity 45, 96
Fanon, Frantz 17
feminism 5–6, 18
feminist: ethics 94, 97, 99–101; killjoy 17, 19–20
Foucault, Michel 37

Garrud, Edith 5
Gherardi, Silvia 7, 69, 76, 78
Guattari, Félix 40, 63, 69

Hamilton, Jennifer 93–94
happy/happiness 12–15
Haraway, Donna 3, 5, 7, 37–38, 40, 45–57
Hawkins, Gay 93, 103
Heidegger, Martin 16, 38
heterosexual 15, 19
Hochschild, Arlie Russell 5, 19
hooks, bell 5
Höpfl, Heather 5
human: being 39, 51, 62, 64, 68, 71; perception 46
humanism 48–49, 56
Husserl, Edmund 16

inequality 5, 9, 66, 101
Influx and efflux (Bennett) 65, 67, 73n1
intensities 33, 38, 40, 63, 77, 79, 82
intercorporeality 96, 99–100
intra-action 41, 77–81, 83, 86, 88
Irigaray, Luce 5

kinship 45, 48–49, 52, 55–57
knowledge: colonial 17; legitimate 24, 34, 46, 54–55; tentacular 47

Latimer, Joanna 45, 52, 93
Latour, Bruno 35, 49, 50, 63
leader 2, 56, 67

leadership 57, 66–68, 71–72
Levinas, Emmanuel 95–96
LGBT+ 23
lineage, conceptual 15, 18, 94

management: affective 3–6, 22; critical 52; traditional 68
management and organizational studies (MOS) 76–79, 88
materialities 38, 48, 77–78, 85–86, 99–100, 103, 105
Merleau-Ponty, Maurice 95
methodology 81
more-than-human 55, 65, 92–94, 104

nature of nature 46
nature/natural 46, 51, 57, 64, 83, 100; organic metaphors 46, 50, 52–53; *see also* bokashi
Neimanis, Astrida 93–94
neoliberalization 80–81
new materialism 5, 8, 39, 63–64, 77
Nietzsche, Friedrich 37, 95
non-human: objects/bodies 1, 3, 5, 8, 63, 67; others 7, 40, 45, 49, 52, 54, 77, 81, 100
normativity 6, 12, 98, 101

objects 20–21, 24, 31–32, 38, 50, 67, 70; *see also* non-human
oddkin 51–52
ordinary 24, 32–33, 40
ordinary affects *see* affects
organizational: analysis 69, 71, 73; ethics 9, 66, 72, 94, 97–98
orientation 16–17, 20–21, 24–25

posthuman 76, 99–101
power: exploitative 53, 98–100; relations 5–6, 14, 56, 99–100; system of 17, 48, 92; thing 63–64, 69; of words 54, 86
privilege 6–7, 98
Puig de la Bellacasa, Maria 93, 100
Pullen, Alison 64–65, 98

queer 17, 23, 25, 84

race 5, 8
racism 25
relationships 1–3, 7–8, 45, 50, 52, 64

responsibility: ethical 8, 68, 82, 97, 99, 103; social 46, 53, 62
Rhodes, Carl 98
rhythm 34

Sedgwick, Eve Kosofsky 5, 40
sexist 19
Shotwell, Alexis 93, 100
spider: legs, unfolding 53; woman 50, 52
Spinoza, Baruch 15–16, 37
stakeholder theory 55
Staunas, Dorthe 86–87
Stengers, Isabelle 37
Stewart, Kathleen 5, 7–8, 29–30, 40
Strathern, Marilyn 40
Strati, Antonio 41

Taussig, Michael 37, 40
Thiele, Kathrin 88
Third World 17
Thrift, Nigel 37
Tyler, Melissa 22–23

Vachhani, Sheena J. 81–82
Valtonen, Anu 64–65
vibrant matter 8, 62, 71
Vitry, Chloé 23
vulnerability 77, 87; *see also* exposed

whiteness 6, 17, 21–23
worlding 29, 31, 35, 37–38
writing differently 7–8, 80–81, 87

Printed in the United States
by Baker & Taylor Publisher Services